MATHEMATICS & ECONOMICS

CONNECTIONS FOR LIFE • GRADES 3-5

This publication was made possible

through funding from the 3M Foundation

National Council on Economic Education

Acknowledgments

Project Director
Mary Lynn Reiser
Associate Director
UNO Center for Economic Education
University of Nebraska-Omaha

Project Editor
Melinda Patterson Grenier

Design
Karl Hartig

Field Test Schools and Teachers

J.W. Baker Elementary School
Little Rock, Ark.

Mildred Baker	Fifth Grade Teacher
Michele Carter	Third Grade Teacher
Jessica Collier	Third Grade Teacher
Peggy Dodge	Fifth Grade Teacher
MeShelle Hays	Fourth Grade Teacher
Kyron Jones	Fifth Grade Teacher
Tracy Tucker	Fourth Grade Teacher

Conestoga Magnet School
Omaha, Neb.

Deanna Adams	Fifth Grade Teacher
Mary Cotton	Fourth Grade Teacher
Tammy Cruz	Fourth Grade Teacher
Karen McElroy	Sixth Grade Teacher
Jennifer Nelson	Third Grade Teacher
Janie Peterson	Gifted Facilitator
Francie Smith	Fifth Grade Teacher
Brenetta Wayne	Fourth Grade Teacher

ISBN   1-56183-536-6

Contents

Authors

Writers

Mary Suiter is the director of the Center for Entrepreneurship and Economic Education at the University of Missouri-St. Louis. She is the author or co-author of numerous economics curricula including *Money Math: Skills for Life, Focus: Middle School Economics, Economics at Work, Money Math: Lessons for Life* and *Mathematics & Economics: Connections for Life, Grades 6-8*. Suiter was a member of the writing committee for the Voluntary National Content Standards in Economics. She served as president of the National Association of Economic Educators (NAEE) and is currently a senior program fellow for the National Council on Economic Education (NCEE). In 1998, she received the NAEE/NCEE Bessie B. Moore Service Award.

Donna Wright is the associate director of the Arkansas Council on Economic Education. She is co-author of *Financial Fitness for Life: Pocketwise* and *Economics and Children's Literature: Storybooks for Primary Grades*. She was a classroom teacher in Hot Springs, Ark., for 12 years before taking the position of economic-education specialist for Pulaski County Special School District for four years. Wright is a national award winner for her work on innovative economic-education teaching units and was instrumental in the development of the Bessie B. Moore Arkansas Awards for Excellence in Teaching Economics.

Susan Hinchik is currently the math specialist at Conestoga Magnet School, a school in Omaha, Neb., that focuses on math and economics. Before becoming the math specialist, Hinchik was a fourth grade classroom teacher. She has also taught third and sixth grades. Hinchik has a master's of education in curriculum and instruction from Doane College. She has also had extensive training in "Investigations," a standards-based math curriculum developed at TERC (Technical Education Research Centers) and is an Investigations trainer for Omaha Public Schools. She is a member of the National Council of Teachers of Mathematics (NCTM) and has attended NCTM academies for professional development in the areas of geometry, algebra and data analysis.

Marsha Strange Masters is the economics specialist at Baker Interdistrict Elementary School in Little Rock, Ark., where she teaches economics to students in kindergarten through fifth grade. In addition, she serves as a curriculum consultant for the Arkansas Council on Economic Education. Masters was given the distinguished honor of being selected a Polly M. Jackson Master Economics Teacher in 2000. Incorporating economics through all areas of the curriculum, she has been involved in a number of interdisciplinary projects with students and has been awarded honors in the National Awards for Teaching Economics and the Bessie B. Moore Arkansas Awards Program.

Michele T. Wulff is the economic curriculum specialist at Conestoga Magnet School in Omaha, Neb. She has worked in the Omaha Public Schools for 28 years as a teacher for fourth, fifth and sixth grades and for gifted/talented students. Wulff was chosen to attend the NCEE Training the Writers Conference in Bucharest, Romania, in 2003. She was awarded the Outstanding Service to Economic Education Award from the University of Nebraska-Omaha (UNO) Center for Economic Education in 2004. She also received the 2nd Congressional District's Outstanding Social Studies Educator Award in 2004.

Content Consultants

Neal Grandgenett is the Peter Kiewit Distinguished Professor of Mathematics Education at the University of Nebraska-Omaha, where he teaches various undergraduate and graduate courses on the methods of teaching mathematics. He is active in the examination of mathematics and technology-related learning environments and has authored more than 60 articles and research papers related to these topics. One of his articles, "Roles of Computer Technology in the Mathematics Education of the Gifted," won an Educational Press Association of America Distinguished Achievement Award. Grandgenett is a frequent presenter at the NCTM Conference. He is a review editor for new curriculum applications and resources for the international journal *Mathematics and Computer Education Journal*. He has received the National Aeronautics and Space Administration Mission Home Award for his curriculum review and development efforts.

Kim Sosin is professor of economics at the University of Nebraska-Omaha, chair of the Department of Economics and co-director of the UNO Center for Economic Education. She is an associate editor of the *Journal of Economic Education*. She served on the Executive Committee of NAEE and chaired the NAEE Technology Committee. She received the 1999 NAEE/NCEE Bessie B. Moore Service Award and the 2002 NAEE/NCEE Henry H. Villard Research Award. Sosin is creator and Webmaster for EcEdWeb (http://ecedweb.unomaha.edu), a Web site providing resources for economic education since 1995. She has published papers on teaching economics in *American Economic Review* and the *Journal of Economic Education* and wrote an invited chapter on using technology to teach economics in *Teaching Undergraduate Economics: Alternatives to Chalk and Talk*, edited by Bill Becker and Michael Watts.

Sosin has given invited presentations on economic education topics at meetings of the Allied Social Sciences Association/American Economics Association.

Project Director

Mary Lynn Reiser is the associate director of the UNO Center for Economic Education at the University of Nebraska-Omaha. She is co-author of several economics curricula including *Middle School World Geography: Focus on Economics* and was a member of the concept team for NCEE's Virtual Economics CD-ROM. She was president of NAEE and received the 2004 NAEE/NCEE John C. Schramm Leadership Award. She serves as the economics advisor to the Omaha Public School district and worked with the district to develop a model economics magnet school for elementary students.

Foreword

For more than 50 years, the National Council on Economic Education (NCEE) has been the nation's leader in getting economics into K-12 curricula of the nation's schools by teaching teachers and equipping them with outstanding materials. Because economics is so important for success in life, NCEE sought ways to ensure that economics was incorporated into teaching and learning in the social studies by providing tools teachers could use to integrate economics into various subject areas such as government, history and geography.

With recent changes in education, NCEE recognized that it is essential to provide teachers with the tools they need to incorporate economics into other subject areas such as mathematics. In 1999 NCEE published *Mathematics and Economics: Connections for Life, Grades 9-12* and in 2002, *Mathematics and Economics: Connections for Life, Grades 6-8.* Now, through the support of 3M, NCEE is able to provide *Mathematics and Economics: Connections for Life, Grades 3-5.* This excellent resource brings NCEE closer to its goal of providing materials to integrate economics into mathematics K-12.

This publication brings mathematics and economics together in meaningful ways so that younger children learn important skills they can use throughout their lives. This book is especially designed to help mathematics teachers answer the proverbial question students ask: "Why do I have to learn this? Am I ever going to use it?" Each of the 12 lessons in this publication involves the students in applying mathematical skills and thinking to solve economic and personal-finance problems of life. Having participated in the activities in this unit, the students will recognize that mathematics, economics and personal finance are important to the everyday decisions individuals make. In these lessons, the students compare income and expenses in a budget to make a decision, calculate the costs and revenue in a production process, compute interest on savings and compute exchange rates for currency. With each of these activities, the students use their mathematics skills and knowledge to solve economic problems and to communicate economic ideas.

Mathematics teachers may ask, "Do I need to take a course in economics to use this curriculum guide?" The answer is, "No." This book was written by master teachers with review and input from experts in mathematics education and economic education. It provides explanations of the needed economics. However, teachers who have questions may visit the NCEE Web site at http://www.ncee.net to find the nearest NCEE state Council director or university Center director who can provide assistance.

Special thanks for this publication go to Mary Lynn Reiser, associate director of the UNO Center for Economic Education at the University of Nebraska-Omaha, for her diligent efforts to insure that high-quality work was completed. NCEE extends thanks to Neal Grandgenett and Kim Sosin, the content consultants for this project, who made certain that both the mathematics and economics content was accurate and appropriate for students in third, fourth and fifth grades. NCEE is especially appreciative of the support of 3M that made this good work possible.

Robert F. Duvall, Ph.D.
President & Chief Executive Officer
The National Council on Economic Education

Introduction:
Why Teach Mathematics and Economics Together?

Teaching mathematics in today's elementary classroom can be both exciting and challenging for an elementary teacher. It can be exciting because we are experiencing a wonderful evolution in mathematics education that recognizes the importance of teaching mathematics in a hands-on, dynamic and applied way. This approach makes learning mathematics fun for teacher and student alike.

Teaching mathematics for an elementary teacher can also be a challenge because the mathematics that should be taught today includes much more than the simple arithmetic that we adults may have experienced in our elementary classrooms.

In the elementary classroom of today, mathematics is a dynamic discipline basic to our information society and includes essential processes such as problem solving, reasoning, communication, connections and representation. (*Principles and Standards for School Mathematics*, Reston, Va.: National Council of Teachers of Mathematics, 2000). *Mathematics and Economics: Connections for Life Grades 3-5* book helps an elementary teacher strive for thoughtful and creative mathematics instruction by providing 12 model lessons for grades 3 through 5 that give students a great context — economics — for learning mathematics.

Recent research on mathematics education continues to confirm that teaching mathematics in the context of an application is highly effective and that significant, worthwhile and grade-level appropriate content can have considerable influence on student learning. (Iris R. Weiss and Joan D. Pasley, "What is High-Quality Instruction?" *Educational Leadership*, February 2004, pp. 24-28). Primary factors associated with effective lessons were student engagement and interaction with the content.

As it does in many sciences, the discipline of mathematics quite naturally represents a "language" for economics. Economics depends on mathematics to represent relationships, solve problems, and communicate ideas effectively. This real-world context provides a great opportunity for elementary teachers to teach their students current mathematics, while simultaneously offering their students a chance to learn some of the fundamental concepts of economics. Thus, the lessons in this book will help teachers illustrate to their students the real power of mathematics in our world.

Economics teaches students how to be wise producers and consumers, lessons they will use throughout their lives. Although the focus of these lessons is teaching mathematics within the context of economics, the teaching of economics is itself essential. Forty-eight states now have curriculum standards at the elementary level requiring that students be taught economics. Teachers often weave economics concepts into the material of other subjects as they seek to fulfill the responsibility to address their district's elementary curriculum. Not only do the lessons in this book teach mathematics in a compelling way, they are also exciting and relevant approaches to teaching economics concepts that students will use for a lifetime.

The lessons have been designed by master teachers, reviewed by content experts, piloted in elementary classrooms and published with a careful attention to the potential excitement and utility of blending instruction for these two disciplines. All lessons include hands-on activities, encourage class discussions and provide many effective questions teachers can use to review and deepen student understanding. All lessons, even the fanciful, are grounded in familiar activities relevant to the everyday lives of students.

Each lesson includes a Web address for all of the activities and visuals ready to print, further connections to other disciplines, additional suggestions for mathematics and economics activities for students, and links to interesting information and resources. Most of all, students will be excited by these creative activities and that will excite teachers as well.

Neal Grandgenett
Professor of Mathematics Education
University of Nebraska-Omaha

Kim Sosin
Professor of Economics
University of Nebraska-Omaha

Content Standards: **Mathematics**

Number and Operations
- Understand numbers, ways of representing numbers, relationships among numbers and number systems.
- Develop understanding of fractions as parts of unit wholes, as parts of a collection, as locations on number lines and as divisions of whole numbers.
- Recognize and generate equivalent forms of commonly used fractions, decimals and percents.
- Develop fluency in adding, subtracting, multiplying and dividing whole numbers.
- Develop and use strategies to estimate computations involving fractions and decimals in situations relevant to students' experience.
- Develop and use strategies to estimate the results of whole-number computations and to judge the reasonableness of such results.

Algebra
- Use mathematical models to represent and understand quantitative relationships.

Geometry
- Analyze characteristics and properties of two- and three-dimensional geometric shapes and develop mathematical arguments about geometric relationships.
- Use visualization, spatial reasoning and geometric modeling to solve problems.

Measurement
- Understand measurable attributes of objects and the units, systems and processes of measurement.

Data Analysis and Probability
- Formulate questions that can be addressed with data and collect, organize and display relevant data to answer them.
- Collect data using observations, surveys and experiments.
- Represent data using tables and graphs such as line plots, bar graphs and line graphs.
- Select and use appropriate statistical methods to analyze data.
- Propose and justify conclusions and predictions that are based on data, and design studies to further investigate the conclusions or predictions.

Problem Solving
- Build new mathematical knowledge through problem solving.
- Solve problems that arise in mathematics and in other contexts.
- Apply and adapt a variety of appropriate strategies to solve problems.

Connections
- Recognize and apply mathematics in contexts outside of mathematics.

Representation
- Create and use representations to organize, record and communicate mathematical ideas.

Selected standards from *Principals & Standards for School Mathematics*

A Correlation of the Lessons with the Mathematics Standards

Standards	Lesson 1	Lesson 2	Lesson 3	Lesson 4	Lesson 5	Lesson 6	Lesson 7	Lesson 8	Lesson 9	Lesson 10	Lesson 11	Lesson 12
Number and Operations												
• Understand numbers, ways of representing numbers, relationships ...	●											
• Develop understanding of fractions as parts of unit wholes, as parts ...		●								●		
• Recognize and generate equivalent forms of commonly used fractions, ...											●	●
• Compute fluently and make reasonable estimates.	●		●		●							
• Develop fluency in adding, subtracting, multiplying and dividing ...				●								
• Develop and use strategies to estimate computations involving fractions ...				●		●				●		
• Develop and use strategies to estimate the results of whole-number ...				●								
Algebra												
• Use mathematical models to represent and understand quantitative ...		●										
Geometry												
• Analyze characteristics and properties of two- and three-dimensional ...							●					
• Use visualization, spatial reasoning and geometric modeling to solve ...							●					
Measurement												
• Understand measurable attributes of objects and the units, systems ...			●						●			
Data Analysis and Probability												
• Formulate questions that can be addressed with data and collect, ...		●										
• Collect data using observations, surveys and experiments.								●				
• Represent data using tables and graphs such as line plots, bar graphs ...								●				
• Select and use appropriate statistical methods to analyze data.		●	●									
• Propose and justify conclusions and predictions that are based on data, ...								●				
Problem Solving												
• Build new mathematical knowledge through problem solving.											●	
• Solve problems that arise in mathematics and in other contexts.	●				●	●				●	●	●
• Apply and adapt a variety of appropriate strategies to solve problems.	●	●			●	●				●		
Connections												
• Recognize and apply mathematics in contexts outside of mathematics.	●	●	●	●	●	●	●	●	●	●	●	●
Representation												
• Create and use representations to organize, record and communicate ...									●			

Selected standards from *Principals & Standards for School Mathematics*

Content Standards: **Economics**

In the Voluntary National Content Standards in Economics, benchmarks for demand, entrepreneurs, profit and losses are at the eighth grade level. Many district elementary economics curricula introduce these concepts in lower grades, so we included them in these lessons.

Standard 1

   • **Benchmark 1 for 4th grade:** People make choices because they cannot have everything they want.

   • **Benchmark 3 for 4th grade:** Goods are objects that can satisfy people's wants.

   • **Benchmark 4 for 4th grade:** Services are actions that can satisfy people's wants.

   • **Benchmark 5 for 4th grade:** People's choices about what goods and services to buy and consume determine how resources will be used.

   • **Benchmark 6 for 4th grade:** Whenever a choice is made, something is given up.

   • **Benchmark 7 for 4th grade:** The opportunity cost of a choice is the value of the best alternative given up.

   • **Benchmark 8 for 4th grade:** People whose wants are satisfied by using goods and services are called consumers.

   • **Benchmark 9 for 4th grade:** Productive resources are the natural resources, human resources and capital goods available to make goods and services.

   • **Benchmark 10 for 4th grade:** Natural resources, such as land, are "gifts of nature"; they are present without human intervention.

   • **Benchmark 11 for 4th grade:** Human resources are the quantity and quality of human effort directed toward producing goods and services.

   • **Benchmark 12 for 4th grade:** Capital goods are goods produced and used to make other goods and services.

Standard 2

   • **Benchmark 1 for 4th grade:** Few choices are all-or-nothing decisions; they usually involve getting a little more of one thing by giving up a little of something else.

   • **Benchmark 2 for 4th grade:** A cost is what you give up when you decide to do something.

   • **Benchmark 3 for 4th grade:** A benefit is something that satisfies your wants.

Standard 5

   • **Benchmark 1 for 4th grade:** Exchange is trading goods and services with people for other goods and services or for money.

   • **Benchmark 2 for 4th grade:** The oldest form of exchange is barter — the direct trading of goods and services between people.

   • **Benchmark 3 for 4th grade:** People voluntarily exchange goods and services because they expect to be better off after the exchange.

Standard 6

   • **Benchmark 3 for 4th grade:** Specialization and division of labor usually increase the productivity of workers.

Standard 8

   • **Benchmark 1 for 4th grade:** Higher prices for a good or service provide incentives for buyers to purchase less of that good or service and for producers to make or sell more of it. Lower prices for a good or service provide incentives for buyers to purchase more of that good or service and for producers to make or sell less of it.

   • **Benchmark 1 for 8th grade:** An increase in the price of a good or service encourages people to look for substitutes, causing the quantity demanded to decrease and vice versa. This relationship between price and quantity demanded, known as the law of demand, exists as long as other factors influencing demand do not change.

Standard 10
• Benchmark 1 for 4th grade:
Banks are institutions where people save money and earn interest, and where other people borrow money and pay interest.
• Benchmark 2 for 4th grade:
Saving is the part of income not spent on taxes or consumption.

Standard 11
• Benchmark 1 for 4th grade:
Money is anything widely accepted as final payment for goods and services.
• Benchmark 2 for 4th grade:
Money makes trading easier by replacing barter with transactions involving currency, coins or checks.
• Benchmark 5 for 4th grade:
Most countries create their own currency for use as money.

Standard 15
• Benchmark 1 for 4th grade:
When workers learn and practice new skills they are improving their human capital.
• Benchmark 2 for 4th grade:
Workers can improve their productivity by improving their human capital.
• Benchmark 3 for 4th grade:
Workers can improve their productivity by using physical capital such as tools and machinery.

Standard 14
• Benchmark 3 for 8th grade:
Entrepreneurs and other sellers earn profits when buyers purchase the products they sell at prices high enough to cover the costs of production.
• Benchmark 4 for 8th grade:
Entrepreneurs and other sellers incur losses when buyers do not purchase products they sell at prices high enough to cover the costs of production.

Selected standards from *Voluntary National Content Standards in Economics*
National Council on Economic Education, 1997

A Correlation of the Lessons with the Voluntary National Content Standards in Economics

Standards	Benchmarks		Lesson 1	Lesson 2	Lesson 3	Lesson 4	Lesson 5	Lesson 6	Lesson 7	Lesson 8	Lesson 9	Lesson 10	Lesson 11	Lesson 12
Standard 1	1 for 4th grade	Choices	●	●							●			
	3 for 4th grade	Goods	●											
	4 for 4th grade	Services	●											
	5 for 4th grade	Choices determine resource use									●			
	6 for 4th grade	Choices require giving up something		●							●			
	7 for 4th grade	Opportunity cost		●							●			
	8 for 4th grade	Consumers	●											
	9 for 4th grade	Productive resources							●			●		
	10 for 4th grade	Natural resources							●			●		
	11 for 4th grade	Human resources							●			●		
	12 for 4th grade	Capital goods (resources)							●			●		
Standard 2	1 for 4th grade	Few choices are all-or-nothing decisions		●		●								
	2 for 4th grade	Costs				●								
	3 for 4th grade	Benefits				●								
Standard 5	1 for 4th grade	Exchange			●									●
	2 for 4th grade	Barter							●					
	3 for 4th grade	Why people trade			●				●					
Standard 6	3 for 4th grade	Specialization and division of labor					●							
Standard 8	1 for 4th grade	Prices provide incentives to buyers								●				
	1 for 8th grade	Law of demand								●				
Standard 10	1 for 4th grade	Banks											●	
	2 for 4th grade	Saving											●	
Standard 11	1 for 4th grade	What is money												●
	2 for 4th grade	Money makes trading easier												●
	5 for 4th grade	Most countries create currency												●
Standard 14	3 for 8th grade	Entrepreneurs, profits						●						
	4 for 8th grade	Entrepreneurs, losses						●						
Standard 15	1 for 4th grade	New skills increase human capital					●							
	2 for 4th grade	Human capital and productivity					●							
	3 for 4th grade	Physical capital and productivity					●							

Selected standards from *Voluntary National Content Standards in Economics*
National Council on Economic Education, 1997

Lesson 1 - A Season of Goods

OVERVIEW

This lesson focuses on goods and services (economics) and basic operations (mathematics). The students review the four seasons of the year and brainstorm goods and services that people often purchase during each season. The students then participate in a matching game, pairing goods and services according to the seasons. Finally, the students work on an activity that requires them to act as consumers on a budget and make decisions to purchase goods and services.

CONCEPTS

Economics
Budgeting
Complementary goods and services
Consumers
Goods and services

Mathematics
Basic operations
Problem solving

CONTENT STANDARDS

Economics
Standard 1
 • **Benchmark 1 for 4th grade:** People make choices because they cannot have everything they want.
 • **Benchmark 3 for 4th grade:** Goods are objects that can satisfy people's wants.
 • **Benchmark 4 for 4th grade:** Services are actions that can satisfy people's wants.
 • **Benchmark 8 for 4th grade:** People whose wants are satisfied by using goods and services are called consumers.

Mathematics
Number and Operations
 • Understand numbers, ways of representing numbers, relationships among numbers and number systems.
 • Compute fluently and make reasonable estimates.
Problem Solving
 • Solve problems that arise in mathematics and in other contexts.
 • Apply and adapt a variety of appropriate strategies to solve problems.
Connections
 • Recognize and apply mathematics in contexts outside of mathematics.

OBJECTIVES

The students will:
1. Identify and sort goods and services.

2. Make choices about purchasing goods and services given an amount of money.

3. Add and subtract three- and four-digit numbers.

4. Apply computation within the context of solving an economic problem.

5. Make decisions as a consumer purchasing goods and services.

TIME REQUIRED

90 minutes

MATERIALS

1. Visual 1.1

2. One copy of Activity 1.1, cut apart to provide a card for each student

3. One copy of Activity 1.2, 1.3, 1.4 or 1.5 for each student in the appropriate group

4. One copy of Activity 1.6 for each student

5. Blank transparencies, transparency pens

ADDITIONAL RESOURCES

For additional curriculum connections, Web links, technology applications and suggested children's literature that will help you teach this lesson, go to
http://mathandecon.ncee.net/35/lesson1/

PROCEDURE

1. Tell the students that they are going to learn about goods and services and the four seasons of the year. Define **goods** as objects that can satisfy people's economic wants. Using goods and services is also consuming them. Ask the students for examples of goods they consume. ***Answers will vary and include pencils, erasers, paper, clothes and food.***

2. Ask the students if people use the same goods all year long. Provide the following example: Do we use a snow shovel all year long? No. Why? Because it doesn't snow all year long in most places.

3. Make four columns on a blank transparency and write one season at the top of each column. Ask the students to give some characteristics of each season. For example, it is usually very hot in the summer and very cold in the winter. ***Answers will vary and depend on the location of the school.***

4. Ask the students if they have noticed that many retail and grocery stores have a "seasonal" aisle toward the front of the store with goods for a particular time of year. Ask the students for a few examples of goods they have seen on sale in these aisles during different seasons. Write the goods in the appropriate column on the transparency. ***Answers will vary and include suntan lotion in summer, mittens and warm hats in winter, garden supplies in spring and back-to-school items in the fall.***

5. Have the students recall some examples of goods they may find in a home closet or garage. Add these goods to the transparency in the column for the season when people are most likely to use them.

6. Write "Goods" at the top of the table as the title. Discuss how people know a good belongs in a specific season. For example, people wear swimsuits in the summer because it is hot and people swim. Remind the students that some people swim all year long in warm climates. Umbrellas are popular in the spring because it rains in many regions in the spring. In winter, sleds are very popular in areas where it snows. Pumpkins are popular in the fall because people use them for Thanksgiving and Halloween decorations.

7. Define **services** as actions that can satisfy people's economic wants. Provide examples of services that the students may have used in the last month, such as haircuts, bicycle repair and bus rides. Clarify for the students that services may involve goods such as rakes, but the action of raking is a service.

8. Point out that people provide some services only during a particular season — for example, snow removal in winter or lawn care in the summer.

9. Have the students brainstorm some examples of services. Write these services

on the transparency in the appropriate column, and add the words "and Services" to the title of the table so the title reads "Goods and Services."

10. Display Visual 1.1. Read through all the items and ask the students to identify each as a good or a service.
Goods: shoulder pads, beach ball, swimsuit, hot chocolate, suntan lotion, garden hoe, flower seeds, sand bucket and shovel, kite, watering can, scarf, pumpkins, wool mittens, rake and snow shovel
Services: sleigh rides, pumpkin carving, snow removal, snorkeling lessons, gardening, lifeguarding, lawn mowing, sailing lessons, lawn raking, house cleaning, football refereeing, tree planting, hay-wagon rides, wood chopping, apple picking, water-skiing lessons and snow-skiing lessons

11. Ask for volunteers to identify pairs of items that go together and briefly explain why they match. For example, flower seeds and a garden hoe go together because people use them together in the garden in the spring and summer.

12. Tell the students that economists call goods or services that go together **complementary goods or services** because people typically consume them together. For example, wool mittens could go with sleigh rides, snow-removal service and snow shovel because people use these items together in winter activities. (**Note:** Make sure the students don't confuse "complement," which means two or more parts that mutually complete each other, with "compliment," which is an expression of respect or admiration.)

13. Tell the students that they are going to play a matching game. You will give each of them a card, and they must first determine whether the item on their card is a good or a service. Explain that there are several matches for each card; some

matches can be goods and some can be services.

14. Tell the students that they will find a match by asking each other yes and no questions about the pictures on their cards. For example, "Am I a service?" is a good question because it can be answered with a yes or no. "What service am I?" is not a good question because the person answering the question has to respond with something other than yes or no. Remind the students that they are trying to find someone who has a complementary good or service for their good or service.

15. Do one sample as a class. Write the word "sunglasses" on a transparency, but don't show it to the students. Have volunteers ask questions to figure out what you wrote. Remind the students that it could be a good or a service. Model answering with a yes or no. If someone asks a question that cannot be answered yes or no, help the student rephrase the question.

16. Have the students stand and form a circle. Distribute a card from Activity 1.1 to each student. Ask the students not to show anyone their card. When all the students have a card, tell them they have three minutes and say "go."

17. When time is up, tell the students to stand in a circle again next to a person whose card might have a complementary good or service for the item on their card. If any students haven't found matches yet, ask them to stand in the middle of the circle.

18. Tell the pairs of students to check another pair and see if their matches work. If each pair agrees, the students stay partnered. If not, they go to the middle of the circle and ask a few more questions of the students there. Allow one or two minutes to do this. If there is an uneven number of students in the classroom, allow one or more pairs to add a third person.

19. Have the students share their paired complementary goods or services, and make a list on a new transparency that groups the pairs by season. Let the class determine if the pairings are valid. *Allow the students to agree or disagree with the pairings. They should be able to justify their opinion.*

20. Using the lists on the transparency, split the class into four groups based on the four seasons, and tell the students to sit with their group.

21. Define **consumers** as people whose wants are satisfied by using goods and services. Ask the students for examples of goods and services they consumed recently. *Answers will vary and include food, pencils, paper, clothes and crayons.*

22. Tell the students they will be consumers in their new groups. They will have a spending plan and perform a series of calculations to decide which goods and services to buy for their season.

23. Distribute one copy of Activity 1.2, 1.3, 1.4 or 1.5 to each student in the appropriate groups. Explain that within their groups, the students will work with their good/service partner to
 • decide which goods and services to purchase
 • explain why they chose these goods and services
 • compute how much these goods and services will cost
 • compute how much money is left
 • explain what they would do with the remaining money

24. Allow time for the groups to answer the questions on the spending activity. Answers will vary, with the following exceptions:
 Fall Scenario: Mike bought a hot dog, a cold drink and a foam "No. 1" finger. How much did he spend? *$11.19* How much money did Mike have left? *$3.81*

 Winter Scenario: How much money did you take on vacation? *$50.00*

25. Ask for volunteers to share their answers. Encourage at least one answer for each season.

CLOSURE

26. Tell the students to go back to their seats, and ask the following discussion questions. The students should be able to appropriately justify their reasoning. The students may also answer these questions as extended writing or journal entries.
 A. In all the season scenarios, you could purchase goods and services. What is the difference between a good and a service? *Goods are objects that can satisfy people's wants, and services are actions that can satisfy people's wants.*
 B. Did your group buy more goods or more services? Why? *Answers will vary.*
 C. Do you think it is a good idea for stores to have special seasonal aisles? Why? *Answers will vary but should include increased sales of items.*
 D. Should seasonal goods and services be available all year long? Why? *Answers will vary but might include responses such as the following: Yes, I think swimsuits should be available all year long because people swim in indoor pools and students participate on swim teams.*

ASSESSMENT

Distribute a copy of Activity 1.6 to each student and review the instructions. The students may do this writing activity as a homework assignment or an in-class assessment.

1. Choose your favorite season. *Summer, spring, fall or winter*

2. Give three examples of goods related to your favorite season that you can purchase. *Any goods or objects appropriate to the chosen season that can satisfy the student's wants*

3. Give three examples of services related to your favorite season that you can purchase. *Any services or actions appropriate to the chosen season that can satisfy the student's wants*

4. Write a paragraph that describes how you would purchase and use goods or services during your favorite season. Include in your paragraph at least three of the goods or services you listed above, and explain why you would buy them. Underline the goods and services that are complementary. *The paragraph should include at least three goods and services the student listed. The student should describe why each satisfies his or her needs, and underline complementary goods and services. Example: I swim a lot during the summer. I can hardly wait for school to get out, because I want to jump into the pool. Every year I have to buy a new swimsuit, because my mom says I just won't stop growing. I really liked last year's* <u>*swimsuit*</u>*; but when I tried it on, I could barely squeeze into it, so Mom and I went shopping. At the store there were tons and tons of really cool* <u>*swimming toys*</u> *and stuff. I begged my mom for some new fins, a snorkel, one of those long floating things and an inner tube that looked like a baby seal, but my mom said I would have to save my own money for those things. I really want that inner tube, and I figure that if I do some extra chores around the house, I'll have enough to buy it in a couple of weeks.*

VISUAL 1.1
GOODS AND SERVICES

Shoulder pads	Sleigh rides
Beach ball	Pumpkin carving
Swimsuit	Hot chocolate
Suntan lotion	Garden hoe
Snow removal	Flower seeds
Snorkeling lessons	Gardening
Lifeguarding	Lawn mowing
Sand bucket and shovel	Kite
Sailing lessons	Watering can
Lawn raking	House cleaning
Football refereeing	Tree planting
Hay-wagon rides	Scarf
Pumpkins	Wool mittens
Rake	Wood chopping
Apple picking	Water-skiing lessons
Snow-skiing lessons	Snow shovel

ACTIVITY 1.1
MATCHING GAME CARDS

Shoulder pads	Sleigh rides
Beach ball	Pumpkin carving
Swimsuit	Hot chocolate
Suntan lotion	Garden hoe

ACTIVITY 1.1 (continued)
MATCHING GAME CARDS

Snow removal	Flower seeds
Snorkeling lessons	Gardening
Lifeguarding	Lawn mowing
Sand bucket and shovel	Kite

ACTIVITY 1.1 (continued)
MATCHING GAME CARDS

Sailing lessons	Watering can
Lawn raking	House cleaning
Football refereeing	Tree planting
Hay-wagon rides	Scarf

ACTIVITY 1.1 (continued)
MATCHING GAME CARDS

Pumpkins	Wool mittens
Rake	Wood chopping
Apple picking	Water-skiing lessons
Snow-skiing lessons	Snow shovel

ACTIVITY 1.2
SUMMER SCENARIO

Directions: Your aunt wants to go to the beach for her birthday, and she would like to take you with her. You want to purchase a few things to make your trip more enjoyable. Your mother has insisted that you must take some sort of protection from the sun. You have $56.75 in your piggy bank. Answer the following questions and show all your work. (Use the back if you need more space.)

A. List your purchases, and give two reasons why you chose each one. Remember, your Mom will not let you go without protection from the sun.

B. How much did you spend?

C. How much money do you have left in your piggy bank after your purchases?

D. What will you do with any remaining money?

Items for Sale	
Beach ball	$4.50
Beach towel	$12.59
Sun hat	$11.99
Swimsuit	$26.99
Swimsuit cover-up	$14.79
Suntan lotion	$5.75
Sand bucket and shovel	$2.29
Beach umbrella	$41.09
Cooler	$10.99
Soda pop (6 pack)	$3.97
Inflatable toy	$6.70
Sailboat rides*	$12.50 / 30 minutes
Water skiing*	$8.50 / 30 minutes
Snorkel lessons*	$25.00 / hour

*You must purchase all services for at least 30 minutes.

ACTIVITY 1.3
FALL SCENARIO

Directions: Mike's friend gave him two tickets to the big football game. Mike invited you to go with him. Unfortunately, both of you have no savings, so you must earn some money to buy refreshments and souvenirs. Answer the following questions, and show all your work. (Use the back if you need more space.)

A. Mike went to the game with $15.00. Use the "Jobs" list and explain how you think Mike earned his money.

B. Mike bought a hot dog, a cold drink and a foam "No. 1" finger. How much did he spend?

C. How much money did Mike have left?

D. You went to the game with some money, but you didn't earn quite as much as Mike. How did you earn your money? How much did you earn?

E. List your purchases and give two reasons why you chose the items you bought.

F. How much did you spend?

G. How much did you have left after making your purchases at the game?

H. What will you do with any remaining money?

Jobs	
Lawn raking	$10.00 / yard
Baby-sitting	$3.00 / hour
Apple picking	$2.00 / bucket
Pumpkin harvesting	$0.10 / pumpkin

Items for Sale	
Hot dog	$2.25
Pretzel	$1.54
Popcorn	$1.23
Cold drink	$0.95
Hot drink	$0.98
Team pennant	$5.50
Foam "No. 1" finger	$7.99
Autographed football	$12.47
Program	$2.00

ACTIVITY 1.4
WINTER SCENARIO

Directions: Your family has decided to take a special trip to the mountains for a winter vacation. You will be staying in a cabin that is near a ski resort in the mountains. You are very excited and decide to bring along some of your own money to purchase some extra items while you are there. You have $100 in the bank, but you take only half of this with you to spend. Answer the following questions and show all your work. (Use the back if you need more space.)

A. How much money did you take on vacation?

B. What did you purchase while on vacation? Give two reasons why you bought each item.

C. How much money did you spend?

D. How much money did you have left?

E. What will you do with any remaining money?

Items for Sale	
Ski goggles	$16.35
Scarf	$7.49
Wool mittens	$5.25
Fur boots	$37.99
Ski pants	$24.99
Lip ointment	$3.20
Ski lessons	$29.90 / hour
Ice-carving class	$8.50 / 30 minutes
Wood-chopper service	$12.00 / bundle
Firewood	$3.00 / bundle
Hot chocolate	$1.25
Snow shovel	$7.59
Map	$2.00
Winter hat	$6.99
Snow-removal service	$20.00 / driveway

ACTIVITY 1.5
SPRING SCENARIO

Directions: Spring has arrived and you are excited about helping your grandmother plant her annual garden. However, your grandmother fell and broke her leg, so she will be unable to do the planting this year. She has decided to put you in charge of the garden, which is 50 square feet, and has given you $75 for the project. Answer the following questions and show all your work. (Use the back if you need more space.)

A. List your purchases and give two reasons why you chose the items you bought.

B. How much did you spend?

C. How much do you have left?

D. What will you do with any remaining money?

E. Draw a picture that shows your garden, including labels showing where you are putting the items you purchased.

Items for Sale		
Garden shovel		$3.39
Garden hoe		$6.50
Watering can		$4.99
Flower seeds		$0.49 / packet
Flowering plants	large	$8.99
	medium	$4.99
	small	$2.99
Wood mulch*		$3.29 / bag
Bark mulch*		$3.97 / bag
Decorative rock*		$6.70 / bag
Garden statue		$12.99
Wind ornaments		$5.25
Gardener		$25.00 / hour
Truck delivery		$15.00
Bird bath		$25.00

*Each bag of mulch, bark and decorative rock covers 25 square feet.

ACTIVITY 1.6
ASSESSMENT: MY SEASONAL PURCHASES

Summer

Fall

Winter

Spring

1. Choose your favorite season.

2. Give three examples of goods related to your favorite season that you can purchase.

3. Give three examples of services related to your favorite season that you can purchase.

4. Write a paragraph that describes how you would purchase and use goods or services during your favorite season. Include in your paragraph at least three of the goods or services you listed above, and explain why you would buy them. Underline the goods and services that are complementary.

Lesson 2 - Choices, Choices

OVERVIEW

This lesson focuses on decision making (economics) and introduces surveying as a method of data collection (mathematics). After analyzing data on a sample topic, the students use a decision-making grid to help them rank career choices and create fractions using the survey data. You can use this lesson as part of a career unit. It focuses on math-related careers, but you can modify it to cover all types of careers if this fits better into the grade-level curriculum.

CONCEPTS

Economics
>Choice
>Decision making
>Opportunity cost

Mathematics
>Data organization and display
>Fractions
>Reading a data table
>Simple mathematical models

CONTENT STANDARDS

Economics
Standard 1
>• **Benchmark 1 for 4th grade:** People make choices because they cannot have everything they want.
>• **Benchmark 6 for 4th grade:** Whenever a choice is made, something is given up.
>• **Benchmark 7 for 4th grade:** The opportunity cost of a choice is the value of the best alternative given up.

Standard 2
>• **Benchmark 1 for 4th grade:** Few choices are all-or-nothing decisions; they usually involve getting a little more of one thing by giving up a little of something else.

Mathematics
Number and Operations
>• Develop understanding of fractions as parts of unit wholes, as parts of a collection, as locations on number lines and as divisions of whole numbers.

Algebra
>• Use mathematical models to represent and understand quantitative relationships.

Data Analysis and Probability
>• Formulate questions that can be addressed with data and collect, organize and display relevant data to answer them.
>• Select and use appropriate statistical methods to analyze data.

Problem Solving
>• Apply and adapt a variety of appropriate strategies to solve problems.

Connections
>• Recognize and apply mathematics in contexts outside of mathematics.

OBJECTIVES

The students will:

1. Explain that people use surveys to collect data.

2. Explain how fractions can conveniently represent part of a unit whole.

3. Give an example of an opportunity cost when making a choice.

4. Generate alternatives and criteria using the PACED decision-making model and make a decision.

TIME REQUIRED

90 minutes

MATERIALS

1. Visuals 2.1, 2.2 and 2.3
   (**Note:** Visual 2.3 and Activity 2.1 are the same.)

2. One copy of Activity 2.1 for each student

3. One copy of Activity 2.2 for each student

4. Internet access or library resources for research on math-related careers. You may also assemble printed information about several careers for the students to use in class or let the students do the research as a class activity.

ADDITIONAL RESOURCES

For additional curriculum connections, Web links, technology applications and suggested children's literature that will help you teach this lesson, go to http://mathandecon.ncee.net/35/lesson2

PROCEDURE

1. Introduce surveying as a method of data collection or gathering information by discussing with the students what surveying means: asking people's opinions, asking how they feel about a topic, allowing them to vote for their favorite choice, asking them what they like best or least about something and asking them to answer questions about themselves such as "How old are you?" Tell the students that collecting and analyzing the results of a survey give people a better idea of other people's choices and characteristics. It also allows people to study and compare these choices or facts. Ask the students if they have ever been asked questions in a survey.

2. Display Visual 2.1. Tell the students that they will learn surveying skills by participating in a simple survey in class. The survey topic will be "What is your favorite school subject?" Ask the students to suggest four or five subject choices.

3. List the students' choices on Visual 2.1. Ask the students to think about their skills and enjoyment of each choice on the list and then vote for their one favorite among the listed subjects, even if their real favorite is a subject that isn't on the list. Survey each student individually to emphasize his or her personal choice, placing a tally mark on Visual 2.1 to correspond to each student's vote.

4. Discuss the survey using the following questions:
   A. Which subject received the most votes? *Answers will vary.*
   B. Did you expect this subject would win? *Answers will vary.*
   C. Which subject received the second-most votes, or came in second place? Third? Fourth? *Answers will vary.*

5. Define **opportunity cost** as the next best alternative people give up when they make a decision. Ask the students if any of them had trouble making a choice because they liked two subjects on the list. *Answers will vary.* Ask the students who answered "yes" what their final choice was and which subject came in second. *Answers will vary.*

6. Tell the students that the second-place subject is the opportunity cost of their decision because this subject is their next best alternative. Explain that when we make decisions, we must give up an alternative we like to select a better alternative for ourselves. Give the following example about yourself:

> If I were taking the school-subject survey, it would be hard to decide between math and language arts [or two appropriate subjects]. My final choice would be math. My opportunity cost would be my second choice: language arts.

7. Explain to the students that they will use the survey results to create **fractions** that represent the opinions of the class about favorite school subjects. Remind the students that a fraction is a part of a whole and that each fraction has a **numerator**, or the number above the line, that represents the number of equal parts of a whole being considered, and a **denominator**, or the number below the line, that represents the total number of equal parts needed to make up the whole. The total number of students in the class who voted will be the whole or denominator of each fraction. The number of students who voted for a particular subject will be the numerator of each fraction. Ask the following questions:

    A. How many votes did the top subject receive? *Answers will vary.* This number will become the first numerator.

    B. What number should be the denominator? *The number of students taking the survey*

    C. Who would like to volunteer to come to the board and write the fraction that represents the number of students who voted for the top subject in the survey? *The denominator must equal the number of students in the survey.*
Continue by asking for volunteers to write on the board the fractions that represent the second-, third- and fourth-place subject choices in the survey.

8. Hopefully, math is one of the subjects the class selected as a favorite. Ask the students if they plan to find a job when they grow up that requires them to do lots of math. Introduce the topic of math-related careers by asking the following questions:

    A. Who can tell me what a **career** is? *A job; work you do when you're grown up* Discuss the meaning of the word career as an occupation a person trains for or works toward.

    B. Why is it important for elementary students to learn about careers? *So they can think about future jobs in which they are interested, develop skills that can help them in future careers and plan ahead for college or training by taking the right classes in middle and high school.*

    C. Do you think math skills and knowledge are important for some careers? *The students should know that many careers require math skills and knowledge.*

9. Display Visual 2.2. Ask the students to brainstorm a variety of career choices for which math knowledge and skills might be needed. List these careers on the visual. *This list can be very long, but if discussion lags you should suggest job titles such as doctor, scientist, salesperson, engineer, banker, accountant and teacher.*

10. Tell the students that their next class survey will be on math-related career choices. Read the list on Visual 2.2 and ask the students to vote for their favorite by raising their hands. Tell the students they can vote for only one choice.

11. Tally the votes and circle on the visual the top four careers. Repeat the exercise of asking volunteers to create a fraction for each of these four careers using the whole class number as the denominator and the number of students who chose each career option as the numerator.

12. Now tell the class they are going to re-examine their top choices using a more careful analysis. This time they will use a decision-making grid: a mathematical table with a number-ranking system that will help them reach their final decision. Then they will see if the decision-making grid makes a difference in the way they rank the career choices.

13. Give each student a copy of Activity 2.1, and display Visual 2.3. Explain that the word PACED is an easy way to remember the steps in this method of decision-making because each letter of the word stands for a step in the process:

    P is the **PROBLEM**: What decision are you making?

    A stands for **ALTERNATIVES** or choices you decide among.

    C stands for **CRITERIA** or standards you use to evaluate the alternatives.

    E stands for **EVALUATION** or judging the alternatives.

    D stands for the final **DECISION** you make.

14. Tell the students that organizing information in a table will help them to make a more informed or thoughtful decision by showing them all of their options and allowing them to compare these options more easily.

15. List the four most popular math-related careers from Visual 2.2 as alternatives in the left column of Visual 2.3 Tell the students to do the same on their copy of Activity 2.1.

16. Discuss the meaning of the term **criteria**. Criteria are standards or measures of value that people use to evaluate what is important. Criteria are listed across the top of the decision-making grid. Ask the students to think of some good standards or criteria that would help them choose among different math-related careers. Write their suggestions on the board. Some examples might be the math skills

needed, enjoyment of the career, amount of education or training needed, amount of money they would make and availability of jobs. Tell the students that the amount of money they would make as a worker is called **income**. With the class, select four of the criteria the students suggested and write them in the appropriate spaces at the top of the grid on the visual. Tell the students to do the same on their activity.

17. Explain to the students that they will evaluate each career alternative separately and rank it according to each criterion, using the numbers 1 through 4; 4 is the highest value or ranking and 1 is the lowest. Then they will calculate the total of the rankings for each alternative and write the answer in the appropriate "Total" square. The alternative with the highest total is the career that best fulfills their criteria and would be their best choice if they were actually trying to decide which of these careers they wanted to pursue.

18. Tell the students that they will need to do some research about the four top careers before they can evaluate them. Have the students work with the selected math-related careers individually or in small groups according to the students' choices, or you can assign the different careers to the students. The students may do the research or you may supply it from Web or print sources. The career information the students research should cover the criteria they selected, which could include schooling required, salaries, availability of jobs and skills or knowledge needed.

19. After the students have done the research as a group project or homework, call the class back together to fill in the rankings. If you assigned different careers to groups, have a representative of each group fill in the ranking for their career. If individual students made their own choices, have them fill out their grids individually. See the sample grid on the next page.

	Criteria				
Alternatives	Interest in Career	Math Skills Needed	Education or Training Needed	Income	Total
Bank Teller	2	4	1	1	8
Pharmacist	3	3	2	4	12
Math Teacher	4	4	4	3	15
Post Office Worker	1	2	3	3	9

20. When everyone is finished, ask them to compare their rankings and then discuss the results:

A. Which career had the most 4s or top rankings? *Answers will vary.*

B. Which career had the most 1s or lowest rankings? *Answers will vary.*

C. Did any career have a mix of rankings? *Answers will vary.* If yes, why do you think this happened? *It was the best choice based on some students' or groups' criteria but not for others.*

D. Which career had the highest total? Which came in second? Third? Fourth? *Answers will vary.*

E. Were there any ties? *Answers will vary.* If two careers tied, show the students how to break the tie by redoing the ranking using only the top two choices.

21. Show the students Visual 2.2 and remind them of the ranking the class gave the four careers before their research. Discuss the following questions:

A. Did their research change the way they ranked the careers? *Factual information about some criteria such as education requirements, income or availability of jobs may have affected their rankings.*

B. Did any of the students prefer a different career after using the decision-making grid? If yes, ask them to explain why. *Answers will vary.*

C. Did the career survey take more time to complete than the first survey on subjects? Why? *Yes, using the decision-making grid takes more time to complete than just making a quick choice.*

D. Do they think the decision they made using the grid was better than the decision they made in the survey on subjects? Why? *Answers will vary, but the students should understand that the grid helped them make a more-informed decision because they carefully considered their criteria, researched their alternatives and made their choice based on how well each alternative met their needs.*

E. Ask a student to share his or her opportunity cost of choosing a career. *The answer should be the student's next best alternative.*

CLOSURE

22. Ask the students the following questions:

A. What is opportunity cost? *The next best alternative people give up when they make a decision* What were the students' opportunity costs as they chose a career? *Answers will vary, but the students should identify their next best alternative as their opportunity cost.*

B. What is a fraction? *Two numbers that relate equal parts to a whole* What is a numerator? *It represents the number of equal parts of the whole being considered.* What is a denominator? *It represents the total number of equal parts in the whole.*

C. What are alternatives? *The options you choose among when you make a decision* Was it hard to choose among your four career alternatives? *Answers will vary.*

D. What are criteria? *Reasons, standards or measures of value that people use to evaluate alternatives.* What criterion did you feel was the most important in making your career decision? *Answers will vary.*

    E. What do the letters PACED stand for? *Problem, alternatives, criteria, evaluation, decision*

    F. How does the PACED model help people make a decision? *It can help people narrow alternatives and evaluate criteria to use. It can help people rank and score alternatives to make a final decision.*

    G. Did using a decision-making grid help you to make a more informed or "thinking" decision on a career choice? Why? *Answers will vary. See the answer to Question 21D.*

ASSESSMENT

Distribute a copy of Activity 2.2 to each student. Read through the directions with the students and allow time for completion. Go over the answers with the students. As you do so, evaluate each student's understanding of the lesson and judge if he or she has listed appropriate alternatives and criteria. Did the students use the grid correctly to make their decision? Did they select the next best alternative as their opportunity cost?

VISUAL 2.1
FAVORITE SCHOOL SUBJECTS

VISUAL 2.2
MATH-RELATED CAREER CHOICES

VISUAL 2.3
PACED DECISION-MAKING GRID

My Math Career Choices

P= Problem or decision you are making
A= Alternatives or choices to decide among
C= Criteria or reasons you use to evaluate alternatives
E= Evaluation or judging the alternatives
D= Decision you make after your evaluation

	Criteria				**Total**
Alternatives					

ACTIVITY 2.1
INDIVIDUAL DECISION-MAKING GRID

My Math Career Choices

P= Problem or decision you are making
A= Alternatives or choices to decide among
C= Criteria or reasons you use to evaluate alternatives
E= Evaluation or judging the alternatives
D= Decision you make after your evaluation

	Criteria				Total
Alternatives					

ACTIVITY 2.2
ASSESSMENT: CHOOSING THE BEST PRESENT

Directions: Use the PACED decision-making grid to choose a gift for a relative or friend.

1. Pick a person in your family or a good friend. Think about items he or she might like, and choose four gift alternatives. Write each in one of the "Alternatives" spaces on the grid.

2. Fill in the "Criteria" spaces with four standards or measures of value that are important to you in choosing a gift. Some examples might be the person's hobbies or interests, the amount you can afford to spend and whether the person needs equipment (a CD player, for example) to enjoy your gift.

3. Complete the grid by evaluating each gift alternative separately. Rank it according to the criteria from 1 to 4, with 4 as the top rank and 1 as the lowest. Calculate the rankings for each gift, and write the totals in the "Total" column.

4. Answer the following questions about your completed grid:
    A. Which gift was your best choice, based on your decision-making grid?

    B. Were you surprised that this gift received the highest ranking? Why?

    C. Which gift was your opportunity cost?

ACTIVITY 2.2 (continued)
ASSESSMENT: CHOOSING THE BEST PRESENT

My Gift-Giving Choices

P= Problem or decision you are making
A= Alternatives or choices you to decide among
C= Criteria or reasons you use to evaluate alternatives
E= Evaluation or judging the alternatives
D= Decision you make after your evaluation

<table>
<tr><td rowspan="2"></td><td colspan="4">Criteria</td><td rowspan="2">Total</td></tr>
<tr><td></td><td></td><td></td><td></td></tr>
<tr><td rowspan="4">Alternatives</td><td></td><td></td><td></td><td></td><td></td></tr>
<tr><td></td><td></td><td></td><td></td><td></td></tr>
<tr><td></td><td></td><td></td><td></td><td></td></tr>
<tr><td></td><td></td><td></td><td></td><td></td></tr>
</table>

Lesson 3 - What's Hot! What's Not!

OVERVIEW

This lesson focuses on exchange and trade (economics) and mean, median and temperatures (mathematics). The students review how to read temperatures on a thermometer and discuss activities associated with various temperatures. They estimate temperatures and find the median and mean of a group of temperatures. They participate in a trading simulation and experience the economic principle that voluntary exchange increases satisfaction.

CONCEPTS

Economics
> Benefits of trade
> Economic wants
> Trade/Exchange

Mathematics
> Estimation
> Mean
> Median
> Reading number lines (temperature)

CONTENT STANDARDS

Economics
Standard 5
> • **Benchmark 1 for 4th grade:** Exchange is trading goods and services with people for other goods and services or for money.
> • **Benchmark 3 for 4th grade:** People voluntarily exchange goods and services because they expect to be better off after the exchange.

Mathematics
Number and Operations
> • Compute fluently and make reasonable estimates.
Measurement
> • Understand measurable attributes of objects and the units, systems and processes of measurement (temperature).
Data Analysis and Probability
> • Select and use appropriate statistical methods to analyze data.
Connections
> • Recognize and apply mathematics in contexts outside of mathematics.

OBJECTIVES

The students will:
1. Correctly read the temperature on a thermometer.

2. Estimate temperatures.

3. Add temperatures, compute the mean and find the median temperature.

4. Explain that people satisfy their economic wants by consuming a good or a service.

5. Explain that when two people trade because they want to, the satisfaction of each person will increase.

TIME REQUIRED

90 minutes

MATERIALS

1.   Visuals 3.1, 3.2 and 3.3

2.   Two copies of Activity 3.1. Make one copy on red paper and one copy on blue paper. Cut the cards apart.

3.   Two thermometers: one inside the classroom and one outdoors, or some other method of reading current temperatures inside and outside

4.   One copy of Activity 3.2 for each student

ADDITIONAL RESOURCES

For additional curriculum connections, Web links, technology applications and suggested children's literature that will help you teach this lesson, go to http://mathandecon.ncee.net/35/lesson3

PROCEDURE

1.   Display Visual 3.1. Ask the students the following questions:

   A. What is this measurement tool called? *Thermometer*

   B. What is the purpose of a thermometer? *A thermometer measures the current temperature.*

   C. What unit do we use to measure the temperature? *Degrees*

   D. Why do you need to know the temperature? *Answers will vary and include knowing what kinds of clothes to wear and what kinds of activities you can do.*

   E. How do you read a thermometer? *Look at the number of degrees that is even with the top of the liquid in the tube of the thermometer.*

   F. What temperature is shown on the thermometer on Visual 3.1? *32°F. Demonstrate how to find the temperature line and read the temperature.*

2.   Write the answer to Question 1F on the board, showing the students how to use and read the degree sign. Explain that people use two scales to measure temperature: Fahrenheit and centigrade. For this lesson, the students will use the Fahrenheit scale. Demonstrate how to write the capital letter F after the 32° (32°F — note that there isn't a space between the degree symbol and the F) Discuss the following questions:

   A. What happens to water at this temperature? *Water freezes.*

   B. How would you dress if you were going outside to work or play? *Answers will vary and include wear a coat, gloves, hat and boots; dress warmly.*

3.   Display Visual 3.2. Ask the students to read the temperature on Thermometer A. *87°F* Discuss the following questions:

   A. How would water feel outside at this temperature? *Warm*

   B. How would you dress if you were going outside to work or play? *Answers will vary and include shorts, sandals, T-shirt.*

   C. What outdoor activities might you be able to participate in at 87°F? *Answers will vary and include swimming, gardening, lawn mowing.*

4.   Ask the students to look at Thermometer B and read the temperature. *18°F* Discuss the following questions:

   A. What outdoor activities might you be able to participate in at these lower temperatures? *Answers will vary and include ice skating, sledding, shoveling snow.*

   B. What is the difference in temperature between Thermometers A and B? *69 degrees*

   C. Which thermometer, A or B, shows a colder temperature? *Thermometer B*

   D. Look at Thermometer C and read the temperature. *75°F*

   E. What is the difference in temperature between Thermometers B and C? *57 degrees*

F. Which thermometer, B or C, shows a warmer temperature? *Thermometer C*

5. Have the class look at all three of the thermometers.
   A. Ask a student volunteer to write the temperatures on the board from coolest to warmest *18°F, 75°F, 87°F*
   B. Ask a student to come to the board and circle the **median** temperature. *75°F* Tell the students that if the amount of numbers listed is an odd number, the median is the middle number. If the amount of numbers listed is an even number, they find the median by adding the two middle numbers and dividing by two.

6. Make sure all the students have a pencil and paper. Ask the class to find the **mean** of the three temperatures. Allow time for computation. Call on a student to write the mean temperature correctly on the board. *60°F* Tell the students that they find the **mean** by adding all the numbers and dividing by the amount of numbers.

7. Ask a student to come to the board and circle the coldest temperature. *18°F*

8. Tell the students to pretend that it is 18°F outside. Discuss the following questions:
   A. If you were outside at this temperature, would you rather be wearing a swimsuit or a warm winter coat? *Most will say a coat.*
   B. Why would most of you be more satisfied with a warm winter coat than the swimsuit? *Answers will vary and include the coat would be warm and protect me from the cold; it would be too cold to go swimming; the swimsuit would not be warm.*

9. Explain to the students that we all have **economic wants**. Economic wants are desires people can satisfy by **consuming** a good or service. Consuming means using goods and services. Therefore, consuming a coat would satisfy their economic want for a good to keep them warm.

10. Ask a student to come to the board and circle the warmest temperature. *87°F*

11. Tell the students to pretend that it is 87°F outside. Discuss the following questions:
    A. If you were outside at this temperature, would you rather be wearing a warm winter coat or a swimsuit? *Most will say a swimsuit.*
    B. Why would most of you want to be wearing the swimsuit rather than the warm winter coat? *Answers will vary and include the coat would be too hot; wearing the swimsuit would help me stay cool.*

12. Tell the students that they have pretended the temperature outside is 18°F and 87°F in the examples they have been working with on the board. Ask them to **estimate** the actual temperature outside the school. Remind them that an estimate is a reasonable guess based on some sample numbers. Would the temperature be closer to freezing water or warm water? *Answers will vary according to the season and local climate.*

13. Ask the students to write their estimate on their paper. Bring in a thermometer from outside the school. Ask a student to read the thermometer and tell the class the actual outside temperature. Have the student write the temperature on the board, using the degree sign and temperature-scale designation correctly. Call on some students to share the difference between their estimate and the actual outside temperature. Did they have a reasonable guess or estimate? *Answers will vary.*
    (Note: If you are in a very cold climate, you may need to discuss with the students what a negative number means and show them this negative number, such as five degrees below zero or –5°F, on the thermometer to help them figure out the difference between their estimate and the actual temperature.)

14. Ask the students whether they would want a coat or a swimsuit at this outside temperature. *Answers will vary according to the season and climate.*

15. Ask the students to estimate the temperature inside the classroom. Will the temperature be higher or lower than the outside temperature? Tell them to write the estimate on their paper. Have a student read the inside thermometer and tell the class the temperature. Ask the student to write the temperature on the board. Call on some students to share the difference between their estimate and the actual inside temperature.

16. Talk to the students about economic wants by discussing the following point: Some goods make us more satisfied, or we have more use for one good than we do for other goods. We could not use the winter coat in warm weather as much as we could use a swimsuit.

17. One way to measure how satisfied someone is with a good or a service is by using a rating scale. Ask the students for a number between 1 and 10 that expresses how satisfied they would be if you gave them an apple to eat. Tell them 1 means not satisfied at all and 10 means extremely satisfied. *The numbers should be on the higher end of the rating scale because most students like apples, but the satisfaction ratings should be varied because some students may not like apples. You can continue the discussion about people being different and having different wants.*

18. Tell the students that we cannot compare one person's rating of 5 to another person's rating of 8 because we cannot really compare satisfaction from one person to another. The rating scale is only for each individual to rate his or her satisfaction. Ask the students how satisfied they would be, on the scale of 1 to 10, if you gave them a lemon to eat. *The num-bers should be lower but still varied because the students are different and have different levels of satisfaction with the same good.* Remind the students that they are not comparing each other's satisfaction; they are rating how satisfied they are with the lemon.

19. Divide the class into two zones, with half the students in each zone (they can stay in their seats). Tell one group they are the Red Zone, and the temperature outside is 87°F. Tell the other group they are the Blue Zone, and it is 18°F outside. Display Visual 3.3. Appoint a recorder for each zone and ask the recorders to go to the overhead. Tell the recorders to write the names of the students in their zone on the transparency.

20. Distribute the red cards you made from Activity 3.1 to the students in the Red Zone and the blue cards you made from the activity to the Blue Zone students. Explain that you are going to ask each of them how satisfied they are with the item they have on their card. Remind them about using the satisfaction scale and that a higher number means they are more satisfied than a lower number.

A. Ask the students in the Red Zone to think about their satisfaction number for the good pictured on the card they are holding. Remind them that the temperature is 87°F and it is very warm outside. Call on the students one at a time to tell you what good they have on their card and their satisfaction number. Tell the recorder to record the satisfaction number on the transparency beside the student's name.

B. Ask the students in the Blue Zone to think about their satisfaction number for the good pictured on the card they are holding. Remind them that the temperature is 18°F and it is cold outside. Call on the students one at a time to tell you what good they have on their card and their satisfaction number. Tell the recorder to record the satisfaction number on the transparency beside the student's name.

21. Ask the students to suggest ways they could raise their satisfaction rating. ***Answers will vary and might include moving to the other zone, altering the good in some way so it would bring more satisfaction OR trading with other students for a good that would bring more satisfaction.***

22. Explain to the students that people often **exchange** goods and services with each other. Exchange is trading goods and services for other goods and services or for money. Tell the students you are going to allow them to trade their good with anyone willing to trade. Allow the students to move around the room to trade for two to three minutes. When the time is up, ask the students to return to their desks. Ask the students the following questions:

    A. How many students traded? Tell them to raise their hand if they traded.

    B. If you traded, why did you decide to trade? Call on the students to share why they traded. ***Answers will vary but should include the idea that they got more satisfaction from the good they traded for than the one they traded.***

    C. If you did not make a trade, why did you decide not to trade? ***Answers will vary and might include no one wanted what I had, I was satisfied with my good and did not see anything I wanted more.***

23. Tell the students that you are going to ask them again how satisfied they are with the good pictured on their card. Remind them that the satisfaction rating is 1 to 10; and the higher the number, the more satisfied they are with their good.

24. Ask the Blue Zone recorder to go to the overhead. Remind the Blue Zone students that it is 18°F outside before asking them how satisfied they are with their good. Ask the students individually what good is pictured on their card and whether they traded. Then ask for their satisfaction rating. Ask the recorder to write the number

on the transparency in the second column beside the student's name.

25. Ask the Red Zone recorder to go to the overhead. Remind the Red Zone students that it is 87°F outside before asking them how satisfied they are with their good. Ask the students individually what good is pictured on their card and whether they traded. Then ask for their satisfaction rating. Ask the recorder to write the number on the transparency in the second column beside the student's name. (**Note:** If a student did not trade, but his or her satisfaction rating went up or down, ask why the rating changed. ***Answers will vary but should include the idea that after the student saw which goods were available, he or she was more or less satisfied with the good on the card. It is also possible that the student couldn't find someone to trade with, and this made him or her less satisfied with the good on the card.***)

26. Ask the students the following questions:

    A. Did some people's satisfaction rating increase? ***If they traded, their number should be higher in Round 2.***

    B. Why did satisfaction levels increase? ***Most of the students who traded were more satisfied after they traded because it was a voluntary trade and they wanted the good they traded for more than the one they traded.***

    C. For all of you who traded, are you satisfied with the trade or would you like to trade again? ***Some will be satisfied with what they have and others will want to trade again. However, the students who traded should have a higher satisfaction rating than before they traded.***

    D. If the thermometer reading is 91°F, would it be more reasonable for you to be skateboarding or snowboarding? ***Skateboarding, because the temperature is too high for snow***

    E. If the temperature is 27°F, would you be more likely to want an ice cream cone or hot chocolate? *Hot chocolate, because it would make you feel warmer*

CLOSURE

27. Review the important content of the lesson by asking the following questions:

    A. What are economic wants? *Desires that people can satisfy by consuming a good or service*

    B. What is exchange? *Trading goods and services for other goods and services or for money*

    C. Give examples of trades you have made. *Answers will vary and can include sandwiches at lunch, baseball cards and clothing.*

    D. Why did you trade? *I wanted what the other person had more than I wanted what I had to trade.*

    E. When two people trade because they want to trade, what happens? *The satisfaction of each person increases.*

ASSESSMENT

Distribute a copy of Activity 3.2 to each student. Tell the students to read and follow all directions. Allow time for the students to complete the activity in class or use it as a homework assignment. Go over the answers with the students.

1. Write the temperature shown on each thermometer.
    A. *88°F*
    B. *67°F*
    C. *28°F*
    D. *76°F*
    E. *41°F*

2. List the temperatures on the thermometers in Question 1 from coolest to warmest. *28°F, 41°F, 67°F, 76°F, 88°F*

3. What is the median of these temperatures? *67°F*

4. Pretend that these five temperatures are from different times of the year in the region where you live. What is the mean temperature for your region? *60°F*

5. Which one of the following goods would you choose to use when the temperature is 70°F? Circle this good. *Answers will vary depending on the students' preferences, but no one should have chosen snow skis because 70°F is too warm for snow.*

6. Why did you make this choice? *Answers will vary and should include something about their choice giving them more satisfaction than the other choices.*

7. How would you rate your satisfaction with the good you chose using a scale of 1 to 10, with 1 meaning not very happy and 10 meaning very happy? *Answers will vary.*

VISUAL 3.1
READING A THERMOMETER

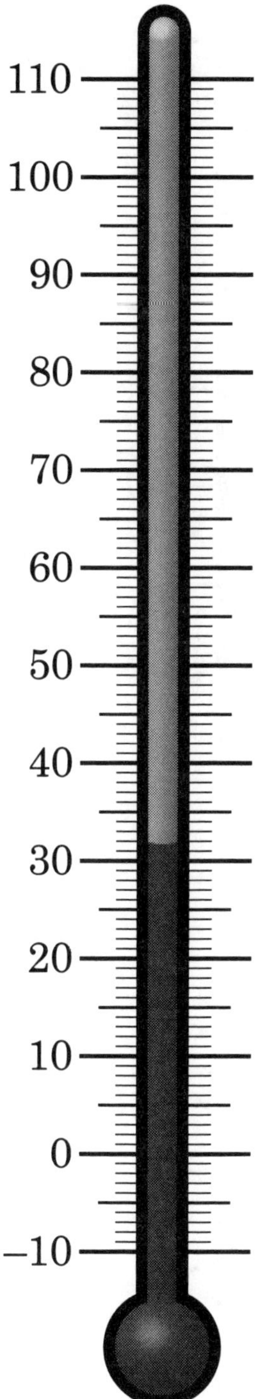

VISUAL 3.2
THREE TEMPERATURE READINGS

A. _______°F   B. _______°F   C. _______°F

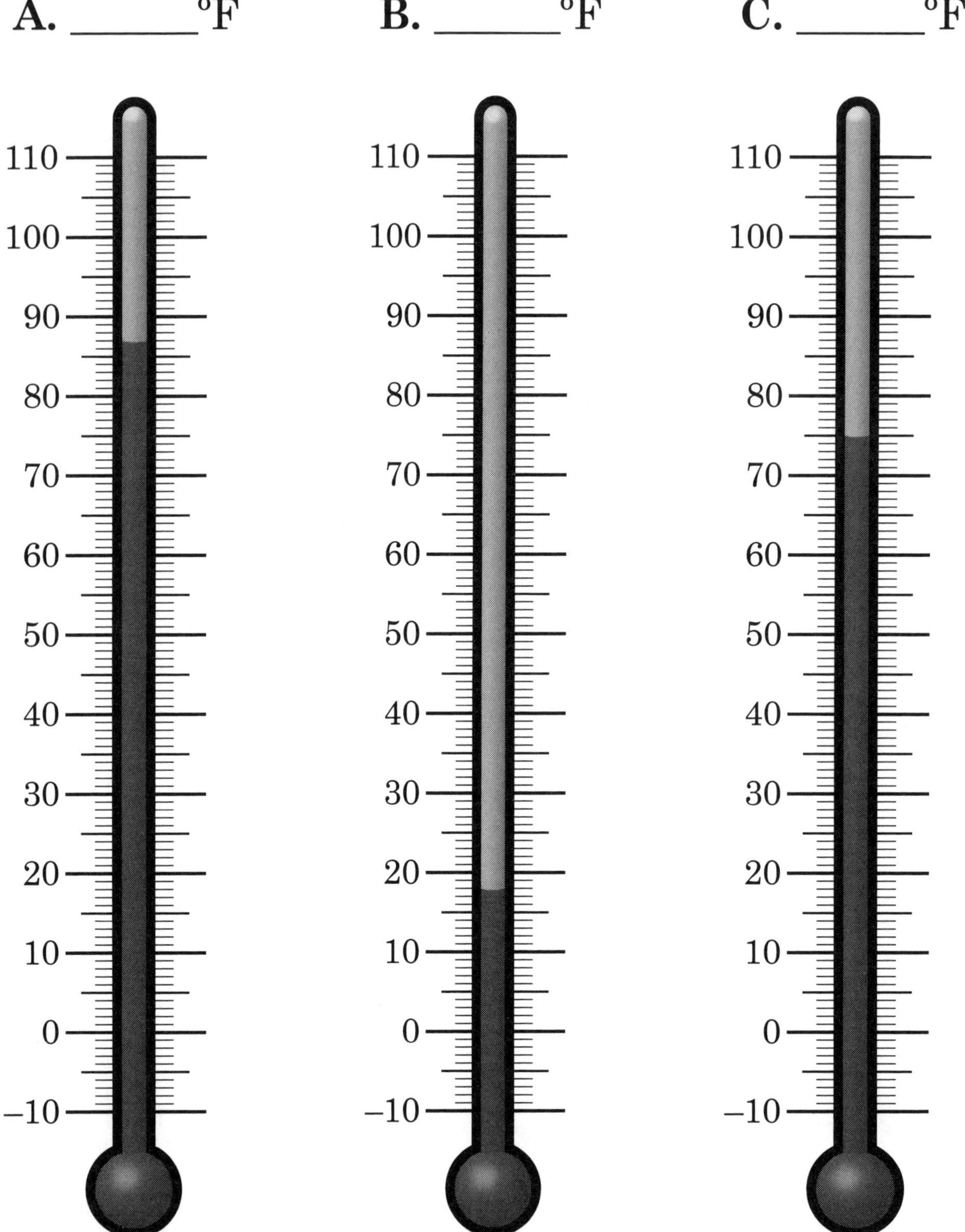

   MATHEMATICS AND ECONOMICS: CONNECTIONS FOR LIFE, © NATIONAL COUNCIL ON ECONOMIC EDUCATION, NEW YORK, N.Y.

VISUAL 3.3
SATISFACTION TABLE

Blue Zone	Rating	
Student Name	Round 1	Round 2
1.		
2.		
3.		
4.		
5.		
6.		
7.		
8.		
9.		
10.		
11.		
12.		
13.		

Red Zone	Rating	
Student Name	Round 1	Round 2
1.		
2.		
3.		
4.		
5.		
6.		
7.		
8.		
9.		
10.		
11.		
12.		
13.		

ACTIVITY 3.1
WEATHER-TIME GOODS

ACTIVITY 3.1 (continued)
WEATHER-TIME GOODS

ACTIVITY 3.2
ASSESSMENT: DO I WANT TO TRADE?

1. Write the temperature shown on each thermometer.

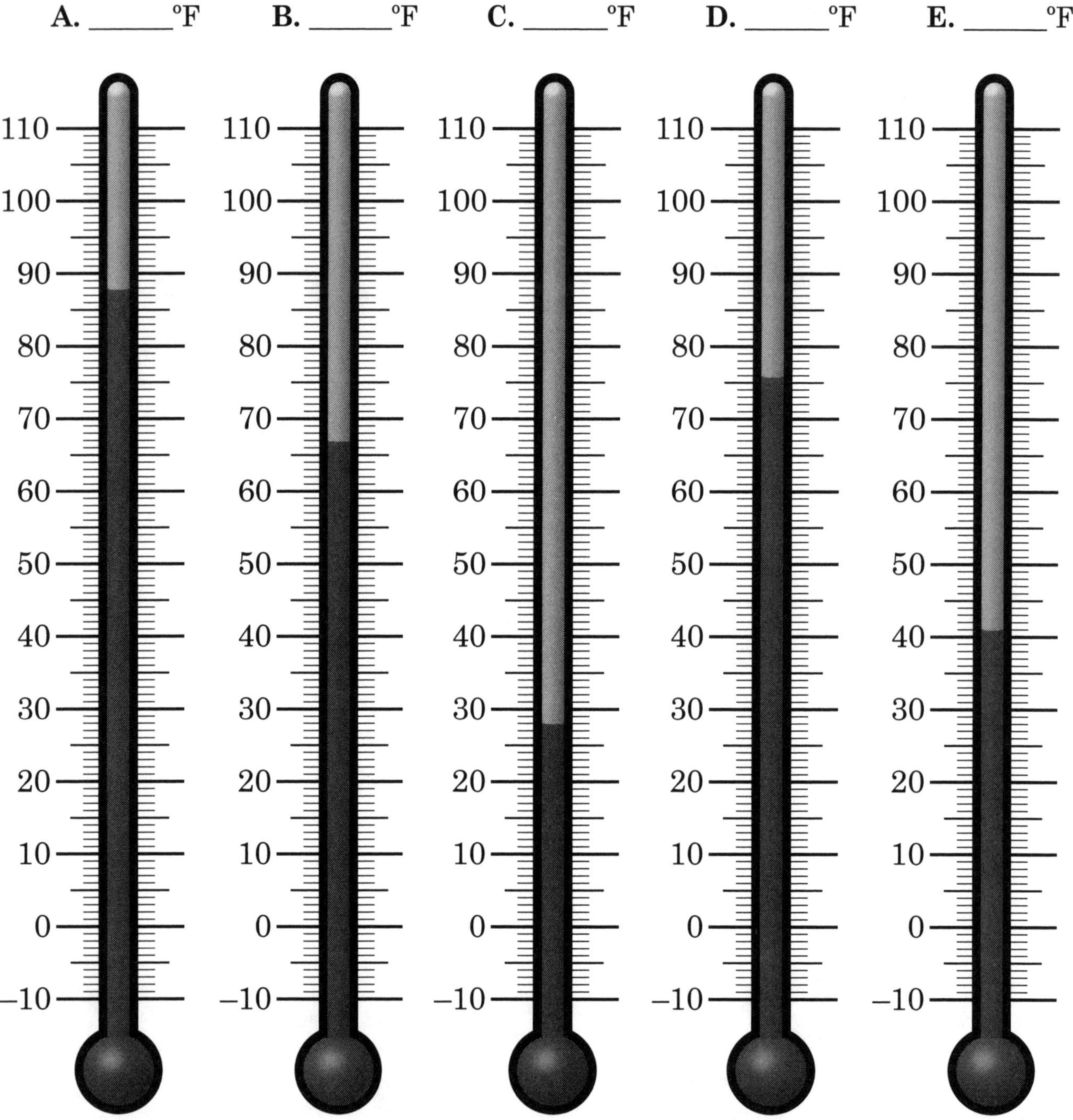

   MATHEMATICS AND ECONOMICS: CONNECTIONS FOR LIFE, © NATIONAL COUNCIL ON ECONOMIC EDUCATION, NEW YORK, N.Y.

ACTIVITY 3.2 (continued)
ASSESSMENT: DO I WANT TO TRADE?

2. List the temperatures on the thermometers in Question 1 from coolest to warmest.

3. What is the median of these temperatures?

4. Pretend that these five temperatures are from different times of the year in the region where you live. What is the mean temperature for your region?

5. Which one of the following goods would you choose to use when the temperature is 70°? Circle this good.
    A. Swing Set   **B.** Roller Blades   **C.** Snow Skis   **D.** Bicycle

6. Why did you make this choice?

7. How would you rate your satisfaction with the good you chose using a scale of 1 to 10, with 1 meaning not very happy and 10 meaning very happy?

Lesson 4 - Pizza on a Budget

OVERVIEW

This lesson focuses on budgeting (economics) and basic operations (mathematics). The students participate in a mouth-watering budget activity while they use estimating skills and practice identifying costs and benefits. Using a budget work sheet, they work in small groups to plan a class pizza party. They review basic-operations skills using money as they make decisions about refreshments for the party.

CONCEPTS

Economics
Benefits
Budgeting
Choice
Costs

Mathematics
Estimation
Whole-number operations

CONTENT STANDARDS

Economics
Standard 2
- **Benchmark 1 for 4th grade:** Few choices are all-or-nothing decisions; they usually involve getting a little more of one thing by giving up a little of something else.
- **Benchmark 2 for 4th grade:** A cost is what you give up when you decide to do something.
- **Benchmark 3 for 4th grade:** A benefit is something that satisfies your wants.

Mathematics
Number and Operations
- Develop and use strategies to estimate the results of whole-number computations and to judge the reasonableness of such results.
- Develop fluency in adding, subtracting, multiplying and dividing whole numbers.
- Develop and use strategies to estimate computations involving fractions and decimals in situations relevant to students' experience.

Connections
- Recognize and apply mathematics in contexts outside of mathematics.

OBJECTIVES

The students will:
1. Practice estimation skills.

2. Design a budget that meets expected criteria.

3. Practice basic operations in calculating expenses.

4. Identify the benefits and costs of alternatives.

5. Use whole-number operations to set up a budget.

TIME REQUIRED

60 minutes

MATERIALS

1. Visuals 4.1, 4.2, 4.3 and 4.4
   (**Note:** Visual 4.2 is the same as Activity 4.1, and both must be prepared ahead of time. Write the names of two familiar pizza locations and one supermarket that sells pizza on Visual 4.2. Write the same information on Activity 4.1 before making copies. If you plan to have a pizza party, you will need to make your own versions of these materials with local pizza options and prices for party items. Visual 4.3 is the same as Activity 4.2, and Visual 4.4 is the same as Activity 4.3.)

2. One copy of Activity 4.1 for each group of students

3. One copy of Activities 4.2, 4.3 and 4.4 for each student

4. Scissors

5. Blank transparencies and overhead markers for each group

ADDITIONAL RESOURCES

For additional curriculum connections, Web links, technology applications and suggested children's literature that will help you teach this lesson, go to
http://mathandecon.ncee.net/35/lesson4

PROCEDURE

(**Note:** In this activity, the students plan a pizza party for 26 students using a $50 budget. All activities are based on these numbers. If you want the students to plan the budget for a real party, revise the numbers to reflect the actual number of students in the classroom.)

1. Tell the students that you have good news. Because of their special effort (examples: good behavior, reaching a class goal), the class gets to have a pizza party at the end of the week. Allow the students to express their reactions to this news. If you aren't planning a classroom party, ask the students to plan a party as practice for an upcoming event.

2. Explain that there is only one stipulation: The class has to plan the party using a budget. Tell the students that a budget is a plan for managing income, spending and saving. Ask the students why someone would use or develop a budget. *To make sure that the person has saved enough money for something the person wants to buy; as a planning tool; as a way to manage income, spending and saving*

3. Display Visual 4.1. Explain that this is an example of a budget. Tell the students that not all budgets look exactly the same. One reason is that some people develop a budget only for themselves, while others develop a budget as a family or group. Review Sam's budget, going over his income and expenses. Tell the students Sam has been working after school and saving his income to go shopping at the mall. By looking at his budget, we can see that Sam has saved for several weeks. He wants to buy a basketball, a CD and a T-shirt and keep a $10.00 balance in his savings account. Ask the following questions:
   A. Did Sam stay within his budget? *Yes, he bought all of the items but still has $10.00 in his savings.*
   B. Discuss some of the choices Sam made because he had to work within his budget. *He had to decide if he wanted a name-brand or a store-brand basketball. He had to choose between a new or a used CD. He had to decide if he wanted to buy a name-brand or a store-brand shirt.*
   C. Review the mathematical calculations Sam used to balance his budget. *Sam figured the total in his savings account: $9 x 5 = $45. He decided to keep a $10.00 balance in the account, which meant he could spend no more than $35.00 on his purchases: $45.00 -*

$10.00 = $35.00. He calculated the combination of expenses that would equal $35.00: $11.02 + $15.99 + $7.99

4. Assign the students to small groups to develop a budget proposal for the pizza party. Tell them they have $50 to spend for the class of 26 students. Their budget must allow for each student to have one 8-ounce soft drink and at least two slices of pizza. They will present their proposals to the class. Each group must be creative and stay within the budget.

5. Give each group one copy of Activity 4.1 and display Visual 4.2. Explain that this is a price list for pizza and other items for the party. Allow the students a few moments to look at the prices. Point out that these prices are not in whole-dollar figures. Therefore, they should estimate the prices to the nearest whole dollar to get a sense of how much money they will spend as they purchase their pizza and other goods: For example, if the price of a pizza is $4.75, the students would estimate the price of the pizza to be $5.00. Ask the students how they would explain estimating to other students who might have difficulty. *One common way of estimating is rounding. If you are estimating $4.75 to the nearest dollar, you would look at the digit in the tenths place. If the digit is five or greater, round to the next dollar. In this case, the digit is 7, so you would round up to $5.00. If the digit is four or smaller, you would round to the lower dollar amount.*

6. Ask the students why or when they might need to use estimation. *If they are shopping and don't have a calculator with them, they would need to estimate to make sure they have enough money to purchase the goods they want to buy.* Allow the students to share examples of estimating they have experienced individually or as a family.

7. Give each student a copy of Activity 4.2 and display Visual 4.3. Tell the students they will use this work sheet to figure out their expenses for the party. Ask the students if they would want several slices of pizza and several cups of soft drink. *Most will probably answer yes.* Explain that their group will have to make many choices because they are working with a limited budget. Review the directions, and remind the students what they must consider in purchasing the pizza, drinks, ice and cups. If necessary, work through an example together to make sure the groups know the processes of calculation.

8. Explain to the students that one way they can make wise choices as they plan their budget is to consider the **benefits** and **costs** of each alternative. Give each student a copy of Activity 4.3 and display Visual 4.4. As an example of evaluating costs and benefits, have the students review Location 1 on Visual 4.2/Activity 4.1. Remind the students that a benefit is something that satisfies their economic wants. Discuss reasons why groups might select this location:
    • The class has heard really good things about this restaurant.
    • It's new and everyone wants to try it.
    • It is running a special on its pizza.
    Remind the students that these reasons are benefits. Tell the students that a cost is what they give up when they decide to do something. Ask the students to identify some costs of choosing Location 1. *Answers will vary and include the following: Maybe the distance we would have to travel to get the pizzas is too far, costing us time and money for gas. Perhaps some people in our group don't want to risk this location because it is so new. They may be giving up pizza they know is good for pizza of unknown quality.* The group will have to make many choices as it weighs the benefits and costs of each location to reach a decision. Tell the students to record these benefits and costs on

Activity 4.3 as they work on their budgets.

9. Remind the groups that each student must receive at least two slices of pizza and an 8-ounce cup of soft drink.
    A. If the group decides to buy one large pizza from Location 1, would this be enough for all the students in the class? *No, one large pizza has only 12 slices.*
    B. Would two large pizzas be enough? *No*
    C. How many large pizzas would they need to buy for each student to receive two slices? *26 students x 2 slices each = 52 slices; 52 / 12 = 4.3 or 4 with a remainder of 4. They would need five large pizzas.*
    D. Ask the students if they could meet the requirement by purchasing some small or medium pizzas? *Yes*
    E. Could they choose to buy some large and some medium pizzas? *Yes*
    (**Note:** Mixing sizes is optional since younger students might have difficulty mixing sizes on their orders.)

10. Tell the students to look at the information about soft drinks on Activity 4.1.
    A. Would one 2-liter bottle be enough for each student in the class to get one 8-ounce serving? *No, a 2-liter bottle provides roughly 68 ounces or only eight full 8-ounce drinks.*
    B. How many 2-liter bottles would be necessary? *Four. The students need a total of 208 ounces of soft drink — 8 ounces x 26 students — and 208 / 68 = 3.06, or slightly more than three 2-liter bottles.*

11. Give each group a blank transparency and markers. Tell them to record their final budget on the transparency, which they will share with the rest of the class. Allow time for the students to work.

12. Ask each group to choose one spokesperson who will present its budget to the class. The spokesperson should explain how the group made sure its proposal met the requirements and share the benefits and the costs the group evaluated. Another option might be to display the group budget proposals for a day and let the students review them before discussing them in class. If the class is planning an actual party, you could ask for a class vote or take the groups' suggestions under advisement.

CLOSURE

13. After the students have shared their budget proposals, ask them to share what they have learned about budgets as a result of this activity. *Accept all answers, which can include the following: Budgets are hard to plan with a group. Our group couldn't have everything we wanted. Some students in our group really liked Location 1 best, but our group chose Location 2 because it was cheaper. After we weighed the benefits and costs, we chose to buy from Location 3 because it was so close to the school.*

14. Ask the students if it was it easy to estimate. (Answers will vary based on the students' abilities.) How did estimation help them work within their budget? *Encourage the students to discuss how estimation gave them a quick idea of how much things would cost to see if their expenses were within the budget.*

ASSESSMENT

Distribute a copy of Activity 4.4 to each student. Each pizza slice represents an open-response writing prompt. Ask the students to select one of the prompts and write an answer to the question on a separate sheet of paper. The students should cut out the slice of pizza corresponding to the prompt they select and glue it to the top of their paper near the heading. Students should write their answers to the prompts in appropriate form. Accept answers that include the ideas listed under each question and other appropriate responses.

1. Someone has asked you what a **budget** is. Why would someone use a budget? *A budget is something people use to make sure they have saved enough money for something they want to buy. It can also be a planning tool or a way to manage income, spending and saving.*

2. What was the most important **benefit** or **cost** your group considered when discussing the pizza locations? *Answers will vary but should give support for the benefit or cost considered.*

3. Explain to someone how to estimate $3.58 to the nearest dollar. (Be specific.) *Look at the digit in the tenths place. The digit is five or greater, so you should round to the next dollar: $4.00*

4. You budget $20 for shopping and want items that cost $4.67, $7.99 and $7.31. How can estimation help you decide if you have enough to buy all the goods? Write in words the process you used. *$4.67 should be rounded up to $5; since the digit in the tenths place is greater than 5, it is rounded up to the next dollar. $7.99 should be rounded up to $8; since the tenths place is greater than 5, it should be rounded up to the nearest dollar. $7.31 should be rounded to $7 since the tenths place is less than 5. Because $5 + $8 + $7 = $20, estimation indicates that there is enough money.*

VISUAL 4.1
SAM'S SAMPLE BUDGET

Sam has been working after school. He saved his income to go shopping at the mall for a basketball, CD and T-shirt. Here are the prices of these items:

	Name brand new	Store brand new	Used
Basketball	$20.02	$11.02	
CD	$15.99		$8.00
T-shirt	$12.99	$7.99	

Here is a budget showing Sam's income from his after-school job and his expenses from his shopping trip:

Income	
Week 1	$9.00
Week 2	$9.00
Week 3	$9.00
Week 4	$9.00
Week 5	$9.00
Total income	**$45.00**

Expenses	
Basketball	$11.02
CD	$15.99
T-shirt	$7.99
Total expenses	**$35.00**

Totals	
Total income	$45.00
Total expenses	$35.00
Left in savings	**$10.00**

VISUAL 4.2
PRICE LIST FOR PARTY ITEMS

PIZZA

Prices are for one topping only and include plates and napkins. Large pizzas have 12 pieces, medium pizzas have eight and small pizzas have four.

Location 1 _______________________
New restaurant, 10 miles away
Large $6.89 *(limited-time special)*
Medium $6.36
Small $4.75

Location 2 _______________________
Supermarket five miles away that sells frozen pizza
Large $6.65
Medium $4.55
Small $3.25

Location 3 _______________________
Very popular place, walking distance away
Large $8.59
Medium $7.65
Small $5.27

SOFT DRINKS

Prices for one 2-liter bottle, which holds about 68 ounces
or enough to fill eight 8-ounce cups
Name brand $1.39
Store brand $0.84

CUPS

Package of 30
Clear plastic $1.55
Decorative $2.19

ICE

For 30 cups
1 bag $0.87

VISUAL 4.3
CLASS PIZZA PARTY BUDGET EXPENSES

Directions: Use this work sheet to figure out your expenses for the party. Then explain your budget on the back of this page: How did you meet the requirements? Will everyone be satisfied?

Goods for Party (plan for 26 students)	Choice of Goods (size and number of items and costs)	Work Space (Use the area below for your calculations.)	Estimated Expenses
Pizza (at least two slices per student)			
Soft drinks (at least one 8-ounce serving per student)			
Cups (one for each student)			
Ice (enough for 26 cups of soft drink)			
		Total estimated expenses	
		Total income	$50.00
		Left over after purchases	

VISUAL 4.4
IDENTIFYING THE COSTS AND BENEFITS

Possible Choices	Benefits of This Choice	Costs of This Choice
Location 1	• Fresh pizza • Special on large size • New pizza restaurant	• Time and gas to get to restaurant 10 miles away • Restaurant is new, so it might not be worth the risk
Location 2		
Location 3		
Name-brand soda		
Store-brand soda		

ACTIVITY 4.1
PRICE LIST FOR PARTY ITEMS

PIZZA
Prices are for one topping only and include plates and napkins. Large pizzas have 12 pieces, medium pizzas have eight and small pizzas have four.

Location 1 _______________________
New restaurant, 10 miles away
Large	$6.89 *(limited-time special)*
Medium	$6.36
Small	$4.75

Location 2 _______________________
Supermarket five miles away that sells frozen pizza
Large	$6.65
Medium	$4.55
Small	$3.25

Location 3 _______________________
Very popular place, walking distance away
Large	$8.59
Medium	$7.65
Small	$5.27

SOFT DRINKS
Prices for one 2-liter bottle, which holds about 68 ounces or enough to fill eight 8-ounce cups
Name brand	$1.39
Store brand	$0.84

CUPS
Package of 30
Clear plastic	$1.55
Decorative	$2.19

ICE
For 30 cups
1 bag	$0.87

ACTIVITY 4.2
CLASS PIZZA PARTY BUDGET EXPENSES

Directions: Use this work sheet to figure out your expenses for the party. Then explain your budget on the back of this page: How did you meet the requirements? Will everyone be satisfied?

Goods for Party (plan for 26 students)	Choice of Goods (size and number of items and costs)	Work Space (Use the area below for your calculations.)	Estimated Expenses
Pizza (at least two slices per student)			
Soft drinks (at least one 8-ounce serving per student)			
Cups (one for each student)			
Ice (enough for 26 cups of soft drink)			
		Total estimated expenses	
		Total income	$50.00
		Left over after purchases	

ACTIVITY 4.3
IDENTIFYING THE COSTS AND BENEFITS

Possible Choices	Benefits of This Choice	Costs of This Choice
Location 1	• Fresh pizza • Special on large size • New pizza restaurant	• Time and gas to get to restaurant 10 miles away • Restaurant is new, so it might not be worth the risk
Location 2		
Location 3		
Name-brand soda		
Store-brand soda		

ACTIVITY 4.4
ASSESSMENT: PIZZA PERFECT

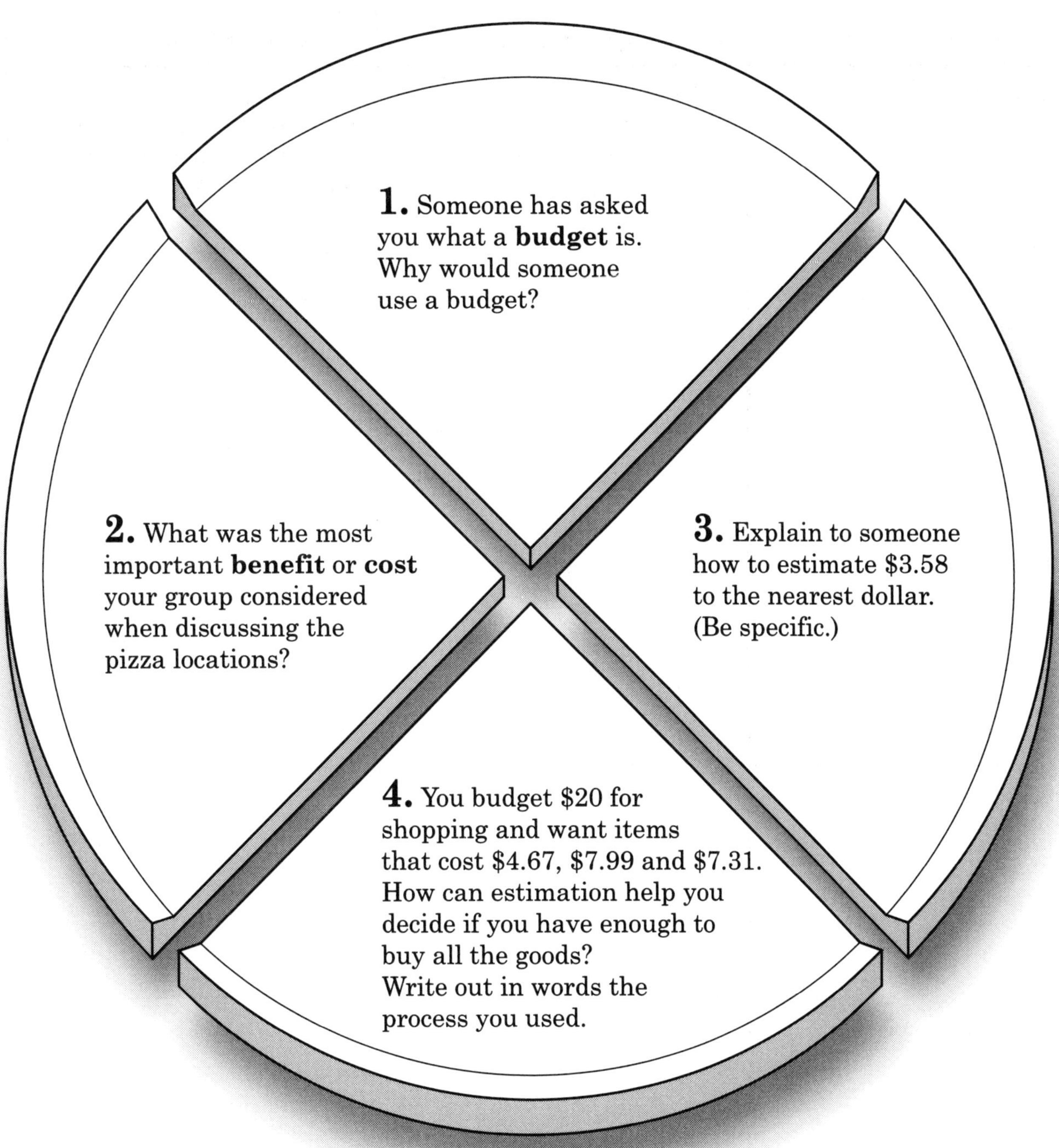

Lesson 5 - The Math Factory

OVERVIEW

This lesson focuses on productivity (economics) and multiplication (mathematics). The students learn about physical capital and human capital as they create multiplication-fact review cards. In the first production round, groups of students produce as craftspeople and as specialists. In the second round, they continue to produce as craftspeople and specialists, but they also receive information that helps them to increase their human capital — their skills and knowledge — and their productivity. In the third round, the students get scissors; and this tool, along with their prior experience, once again increases their human capital and productivity.

CONCEPTS

Economics
Capital good
Division of labor
Human capital
Input
Output
Physical capital
Productivity
Specialization

Mathematics
Multiplication of whole numbers
Multiplication and division terminology (factor, product, divisor, dividend, quotient)

CONTENT STANDARDS

Economics
Standard 6
- **Benchmark 3 for 4th grade:** Specialization and division of labor usually increase the productivity of workers.

Standard 15
- **Benchmark 1 for 4th grade:** When workers learn and practice new skills they are improving their human capital.
- **Benchmark 2 for 4th grade:** Workers can improve their productivity by improving their human capital.
- **Benchmark 3 for 4th grade:** Workers can improve their productivity by using physical capital such as tools and machinery.

Mathematics
Number and Operations
- Compute fluently and make reasonable estimates.

Problem Solving
- Solve problems that arise in mathematics and in other contexts.
- Apply and adapt a variety of appropriate strategies to solve problems.

Connections
- Recognize and apply mathematics in contexts outside of mathematics.

OBJECTIVES

The students will:
1. Define productivity as a measure of output (goods and services) per unit of input (workers and tools) during a specified period of time.

2. Give examples of factors that increase productivity.

3. Define human capital, investment in human capital and investment in capital goods.

4. List the fact families for 2 and 3 up to 2 x 10 and 3 x 10.

5. Use the terms factor, product, divisor, dividend and quotient correctly in completing this activity.

TIME REQUIRED

90 minutes

MATERIALS

1. Visuals 5.1 and 5.2

2. One copy of Activity 5.1 for each group of four to five students

3. One copy of Activity 5.2 for each student

4. Markers and scissors for each student

5. Large supply of index cards or sheets of paper cut to 3" x 5"

6. Transparency markers

ADDITIONAL RESOURCES

For additional curriculum connections, Web links, technology applications and suggested children's literature that will help you teach this lesson, go to http://mathandecon.ncee.net/35/lesson5

PROCEDURE

(**Note:** This activity reviews the multiplication factors for 2 and 3. You may substitute higher-number multiplication fact families or more family groups to increase the difficulty level.)

1. Tell the students they will work in groups to produce multiplication-fact review cards. When production is finished, they can use the cards for review.

2. Demonstrate how to produce a set of review cards using the steps below. Explain that these five cards are a completed set. Ask the students if they have questions. Review as necessary to make sure everyone understands the process.
    • Fold three index cards in half vertically. Tear each card in half along the folded line to make two 3" x 2.5" rectangles. Tell the students each card represents a different part of a multiplication problem.
    • Write **2**, a factor, on a card.
    • Write **x**, a multiplication sign, on another card.
    • Write **4**, a factor, on another card.
    • Write **=**, the equal sign, on a card.
    • Write **8**, the product, on a card.

3. Divide the class in half. Organize each half into groups of four to five students, and give each group a number. Explain that the groups in one half of the class will work as craftspeople. These students will produce their review cards start-to-finish by themselves and contribute their completed sets to the group total. The remaining half of the class will work in their groups as a team and use **division of labor** and **specialization** to produce their review cards. Each person in these groups will perform only one of the tasks required to produce the cards: folding, tearing or marking numbers. Tell the students that producers often use division of labor to produce outputs. The jobs are divided among the workers so that each worker specializes in doing one part of the production process.

4. Tell the students they will have five minutes to complete as many sets of review cards as possible. Their cards should review the 2 and 3 multiplication facts. For example, the students could create the fact families for 2, starting with 2 x 0 = 0, then 2 x 1 = 2, following the pattern up to 2 x 10 = 20. The students could also produce the fact families for 3 using the same process. Allow time for the students to organize their cards and markers. (**Note:** The students may also create fact families for higher numbers such as 4 or 5. The teacher will need to prepare a different version of Activity 5.1 with these multiplication facts.)

5. Allow five minutes for the students to work. When the time is up, check the sets of review cards to be sure that each problem is correct.
(**Note:** You may select a student who is very good at mathematics to assist you, especially with the craft groups.)

6. Display Visual 5.1. Have each group count and report the number of sets that its craftspeople or team correctly completed. Record each group's number, production process and total output, or number of correctly completed sets, in the appropriate columns.

7. Explain that **productivity** is a measure of output (goods and services) per unit of input (workers and tools) during a specified period of time. In this activity, the output is correct sets of review cards, and the inputs are the workers and the tools the workers use to produce the cards. Explain that the numbers you recorded on the visual represent the total number of correct sets of cards, or the total output each group produced in five minutes.

8. Tell the students that they are going to compute the worker productivity for their group. To do this, they must divide their group's total output by the total number of workers in the group. Point out that their output is the dividend in this relationship and the number of workers is the divisor. The answer — in this case, the worker productivity — is the quotient. Have the students do the calculation. Check and record the answers for each group on the appropriate columns of the visual. Have the students put aside their completed correct sets of review cards.

9. Tell the students that they will now participate in a second production round. In this round, they will have more information that should help them produce sets of review cards more quickly. Give each student a copy of Activity 5.1. Explain that this handout provides accurate 2 and 3

multiplication facts. Review the handout with the students and discuss the following questions:

A. What natural pattern exists in the 2 multiplication family? *Moving from 2 x 0 to 2 x 1 and so on, each answer increases by 2. Moving from 2 x 10 to 2 x 9 and so on, each answer decreases by 2.*

B. If you read the products, or answers, moving from 2 x 0 to 2 x 1 and so on, what are you able to do? *Count by 2s*

C. What natural pattern exists in the 3 multiplication family? *Moving from 3 x 0 to 3 x 1 and so on, each answer increases by 3. Moving from 3 x 10 to 3 x 9 and so on, each answer decreases by 3.*

D. If you read the products, or answers, moving from 3 x 0 to 3 x 1 and so on, what are you able to do? *Count by 3s*

E. What is another way to express 3 x 4? *3 + 3 + 3 + 3 or 4 + 4 + 4*

F. What is another way to express 2 x 5? *2 + 2 + 2 + 2 + 2 or 5 + 5*

10. Tell the class that the students who worked as craftspeople in the first round will continue to work as craftspeople in this round. The students who worked in groups dividing labor will continue to divide labor in this round. Allow time for the students to discuss their production processes. Replenish their stock of index cards. Then allow another five-minute production round.

11. When the time is up, check the sets of review cards to be sure that each problem is correct. Have each group count and report the number of sets it correctly completed. Record the information on Visual 5.1. Have the students put aside the completed correct sets.

12. Have each group calculate its productivity for Round 2 and report its answer. Record answers on Visual 5.1. Ask the students if their productivity improved when they used the multiplication-facts handout.

Were they faster and more accurate in the second round? *Answers will vary, but everyone, including the craftspeople, should report that they were faster, more accurate and more productive in the second round.*

13. Tell the students they will have one more chance to produce correct sets of review cards. This time they will have a tool — **physical capital** — a capital good that will help them make the sets more quickly. Give each student a pair of scissors.

14. Tell the class that the students who worked as craftspeople in the first two rounds will continue to work as craftspeople in this round. The students who worked in groups dividing labor will continue to divide labor in this round. Allow time for the students to discuss their production processes. Replenish their stock of index cards. Then allow another five-minute production round.

15. When the time is up, check the sets of review cards to be sure each problem is correct. Have each group count and report the number of sets it correctly completed. Record the information on Visual 5.1.

16. Have each group calculate its productivity and report its answer. Record answers on Visual 5.1.

17. Discuss the following questions:
    A. In the first production round, which groups were more productive? *Probably the groups using division of labor and specialization*
    B. In the second production round, what happened to the productivity for all groups? Why? *Productivity for all groups should have increased. The workers had practice producing review cards and they also had information — the list of multiplication facts — that helped them make more cards in the same amount of time.*
    C. In the third production round,

what happened to the productivity for all groups? Why? *Again, productivity should have increased for everyone. The workers had scissors — a tool or capital good — that allowed them to be more productive.*

18. Explain that this activity demonstrates three ways businesses can increase their productivity. Display Visual 5.2 and discuss the following points:
    • Productivity is a measure of output per unit of input during a specified period of time. In this activity, we measured the output of correct review cards compared to the number of workers in each group during a five-minute production period.
    • Businesses can increase productivity by using division of labor and specialization as their method of production. In this activity, the groups that worked as a team used this method: Each student completed one task in the production process. As the students practiced, they became very good at this one task and could do it faster and better. Ask the students for other examples that show how division of labor can increase productivity. *Answers will vary and could include having different people make and sell hamburgers in fast-food restaurants and having people with different skills play different positions in sports: quarterback and tackle on a football team.*
    • Businesses can increase productivity by investing in **human capital**. Human capital is the skills, education and talent a person possesses. When people practice skills, study information and attend school, they invest in their human capital. In the second production round, workers were given information — a list of multiplication facts — to use. This helped them produce more correct review cards. From Round 1 to Round 2 and from Round 2 to Round 3, workers also practiced, so their output improved. Ask the students what they can do to increase their own human capital. *Answers will vary and can include practicing a musical instru-*

ment or sport, studying a foreign language and going to college or a technical school.

• Businesses can increase productivity by investing in **capital goods**. When firms buy tools, machines and equipment, the workers can have more output in the same amount of time. In this activity, workers were given scissors, a tool that made production of cards faster and easier. Ask the students for examples of other tools and machines that can make workers more productive. *Answers will vary and could include specialized drink-dispensing and cooking equipment in fast-food restaurants, robots in assembly plants, computers in offices and factories.*

19. Have the groups organize all their completed sets of review cards into fact families. There should be enough for each student to have a packet. The students can use these for review by shuffling the cards and then placing them in order to create correct problems. The students in a lower grade level could also use these cards for practice.

CLOSURE

20. Review the important content of the lesson by asking the following questions:

A. What is productivity? *A measure of output per unit of input during a specified period of time*

B. How can businesses increase productivity? *By investing in human capital, investing in capital goods or tools, and/or using division of labor and specialization*

C. What is division of labor? *Each person specializes in only one task needed to make a product, which usually causes the person to become more skilled at the task.*

D. How is production that uses craftspeople different from production that uses division of labor? *With division of labor, each person specializes in only one task. With craftspeople, a single person performs all the tasks needed to make a product.*

E. What is human capital? *The skills, education and talent a person possesses*

F. Give examples of ways to invest in human capital. *Answers will vary and include study, practice, go to school, receive on-the-job training.*

G. If there are five workers in a factory and they produce 20 chairs in an hour, what is their productivity? *20/5 = 4*

H. How would this answer change if productivity increased, but the number of workers and the amount of time remained the same? *The output, which is the dividend, must increase.*

I. In multiplication, what is a factor? What is the product? *A factor is one of the two numbers in the problem. The product is the answer you get when you multiply the two factors.*

J. In division, what is the dividend? What is the divisor? What is the quotient? *The dividend is a number that you divide by another number. The divisor is the number you divide into the dividend. The quotient is the answer you get from the division problem.*

ASSESSMENT

Distribute a copy of Activity 5.2 to each student. Review the directions. Allow time for the students to work. Go over the answers with the students.

1. Read the paragraph below and answer the questions that follow.

     A. What is the productivity of Mr. Simpson's workers in one hour? Please show your work. *The workers' productivity is 10 T-shirts an hour: 80/8 = 10*

     B. Is Mr. Simpson using division of labor and specialization or craftspeople in his factory? *Division of labor and specialization*

     C. What else could Mr. Simpson do to increase the workers' productivity? *He could provide training and practice for his workers; both are investments in human capital. Mr. Simpson could buy capital goods such as computerized sewing machines that help his workers produce more in the same amount of time.*

     D. If the eight workers in Mr. Simpson's factory produced 120 T-shirts in an hour, what would their productivity be? Is this an increase or decrease in productivity? Please show your work. *The workers' productivity is 15 T-shirts an hour: 120/8 = 15. This is an increase in productivity from 10 shirts an hour.*

2. Use the words in the word bank below to complete the sentences that follow.

     A. If you practice and study mathematics so that you understand it and are able to work problems quickly, you are making an *investment in human capital*.

     B. Neal produces 60 candy bars in an hour. This is his *productivity*.

     C. Susie, Tanya, Kevin, Kim and Saul were making cookies. Susie mixed the cookie dough. Tanya rolled the dough out. Kevin cut the dough into shapes. Kim put the cookies in the oven. Saul removed the cookies and placed them on a rack to cool. This is an example of producing using *division of labor*.

     D. Your skills, education and talent are your *human capital*.

     E. Mr. Simpson bought a new machine to produce T-shirts. This is an *investment in capital goods*.

VISUAL 5.1
CLASS PRODUCTIVITY

Group Number	Production Process Craftspeople or Division of Labor	Total Output (Dividend) Round			Number of Workers (Divisor)	Productivity (Quotient) Round		
		1	2	3		1	2	3

VISUAL 5.2
PRODUCTIVITY

Productivity is a measure of output (goods and services) per unit of input (workers and tools) during a
specified period of time.

An increase in worker productivity means
* producing more output (cakes) with the same
number of workers (bakers) in the same amount
of time.

OR

* producing the same amount of output (cakes)
with fewer workers (bakers) in the same amount
of time.

Businesses can increase productivity by
* using division of labor and specialization
* investing in human capital
* investing in physical capital, or capital goods

ACTIVITY 5.1
AMAZING MULTIPLICATION FACTS

2 x 0 = **0**		3 x 0 = **0**
2 x 1 = **2**		3 x 1 = **3**
2 x 2 = **4**		3 x 2 = **6**
2 x 3 = **6**		3 x 3 = **9**
2 x 4 = **8**		3 x 4 = **12**
2 x 5 = **10**		3 x 5 = **15**
2 x 6 = **12**		3 x 6 = **18**
2 x 7 = **14**		3 x 7 = **21**
2 x 8 = **16**		3 x 8 = **24**
2 x 9 = **18**		3 x 9 = **27**
2 x 10 = **20**		3 x 10 = **30**

ACTIVITY 5.2
ASSESSMENT: MR. SIMPSON'S T-SHIRTS

1. Read the paragraph below and answer the questions that follow.

Mr. Simpson owns a business producing T-shirts for sports teams. He has eight people working for him in his factory. In one hour, his employees can produce 80 T-shirts. Each worker performs only one task necessary to make the shirts. Mr. Simpson found that this increases his workers' productivity, and now he is looking for other things he can do to improve the workers' productivity.

    A. What is the productivity of Mr. Simpson's workers in one hour? Please show your work.

    B. Is Mr. Simpson using division of labor and specialization or craftspeople in his factory?

    C. What else could Mr. Simpson do to increase the workers' productivity?

    D. If the eight workers in Mr. Simpson's factory produced 120 T-shirts in an hour, what would their productivity be? Is this an increase or decrease in productivity? Please show your work.

ACTIVITY 5.2 (continued)
ASSESSMENT: MR. SIMPSON'S T-SHIRTS

2. Use the words in the word bank below to complete the sentences.

investment in human capital

human capital

investment in capital goods

division of labor

productivity

A. If you practice and study mathematics so that you understand it and are able to work problems quickly, you are making an

____ .

B. Neal produces 60 candy bars in an hour. This is his

____ .

C. Susie, Tanya, Kevin, Kim and Saul were making cookies. Susie mixed the cookie dough. Tanya rolled the dough out. Kevin cut the dough into shapes. Kim put the cookies in the oven. Saul removed the cookies and placed them on a rack to cool. This is an example of producing using

____ .

D. Your skills, education and talent are your

____ .

E. Mr. Simpson bought a new machine to produce T-shirts. This is an

____ .

Lesson 6 - Bookmark Profit

OVERVIEW

This lesson focuses on profit (economics) and basic operations (mathematics). Working in small groups, the students act as companies and produce bookmarks. They decide which resources to purchase to produce their bookmarks. They calculate their costs of production and display their bookmarks for the class. The students then act as consumers and "buy" bookmarks. Based on their "sales," the student companies compute their profit or loss.

CONCEPTS

Economics
> Costs of production
> Entrepreneur
> Profit and loss
> Revenue

Mathematics
> Addition, subtraction and multiplication
>> of decimals
> Equations
> Inequalities

CONTENT STANDARDS

Economics
Standard 14
The Voluntary National Content Standards in Economics place the benchmarks for entrepreneurs, profit and losses at the 8th grade level. Many district elementary economics curricula introduce these concepts in the lower grades, so we have chosen to include them in this lesson.
- **Benchmark 3 for 8th grade:** Entrepreneurs and other sellers earn profits when buyers purchase the products they sell at prices high enough to cover the costs of production.
- **Benchmark 4 for 8th grade:** Entrepreneurs and other sellers incur losses when buyers do not purchase products they sell at prices high enough to cover the costs of production.

Mathematics
Number and Operations
- Develop and use strategies to estimate computations involving fractions and decimals in situations relevant to students' experience.
Problem Solving
- Solve problems that arise in mathematics and in other contexts.
- Apply and adapt a variety of appropriate strategies to solve problems.
Connections
- Recognize and apply mathematics in contexts outside of mathematics.

OBJECTIVES

The students will:
1. Define entrepreneurs, revenue, costs of production and profit.

2. Explain that profit is income for an entrepreneur.

3. Calculate profit and loss.

4. Explain that profit occurs when total revenue is greater than total costs of production and loss occurs when total revenue is less than total costs of production.

TIME REQUIRED

120 minutes

MATERIALS

1. Visuals 6.1 and 6.2
   (**Note:** Visual 6.1 is the same as Activity 6.3.)

2. One copy of Activities 6.1, 6.5 and 6.6 for each student

3. A resource bag for each group of students that contains craft items such as paper, glue stick, scissors, lace, pipe cleaners, stickers, yarn, ribbon and fringe balls. To figure out how many groups you will have, divide the number of students in the class by four or five.

4. One copy of Activity 6.2 for each student group. Before making the copies, be sure the bookmark resource price list includes only the resources in the bags and an estimated price for each resource.

5. One copy of Activity 6.3 for each group

6. Enough copies of Activity 6.4 to provide three $1.00 bills for each student

7. One blank piece of notebook or copy paper for each group

ADDITIONAL RESOURCES

For additional curriculum connections, Web links, technology applications and suggested children's literature that will help you teach this lesson, go to
http://mathandecon.ncee.net/35/lesson6

PROCEDURE

PART 1

1. Explain that in this lesson, small groups of students will operate a bookmark business. To do this, they must know how to add, subtract and multiply decimals using money. Distribute a copy of Activity 6.1 to each student. Have the students complete the problems, showing their work. When everyone has finished, ask for volunteers to come to the board and demonstrate how they solved the problems.

   A. Suppose you have been saving your money to buy a new bicycle. The price of the bicycle is $175.50. You have saved $75.25. How much more money must you save? *$100.25*

   B. You can walk the neighbor's dog for three days. She will pay you $3.00 a day. If you take the job, how much will you earn? *$9.00* If you put all of your earnings in your savings account, how much will you still need to buy the bike? *$91.25*

   C. Your sister is selling lemonade. The price is $0.15 a cup. If she sells four cups, how much money will she have? *$0.60*

   D. You bought candy at a store. You paid $0.15 for gooey worms, $0.20 for jelly beans and $0.07 for sour stars. What is the total you spent? *$0.42* If you paid with a $1.00 bill, how much change will you receive? *$0.58*
   (**Note:** Review addition, subtraction and multiplication with money as needed. The students could also do this worksheet as homework the day before the lesson.)

2. Ask the students if they have ever sold lemonade or ice water or another product at a neighborhood stand. Explain that you will read them a story about two children who were selling lemonade. Read the following story:

   On Saturday afternoon, Jamal and Sally, two of the neighborhood children, opened a lemonade stand. Mrs. Counts, a mathematics teacher at their school, stopped to buy some lemonade. The lemonade was only $0.25 for an 8-ounce cup.

Mrs. Counts thought this was very inexpensive. She asked Jamal and Sally how much profit they were earning for each cup of lemonade they sold. Jamal told Mrs. Counts that they were earning $0.25 profit. Mrs. Counts was surprised. She asked Jamal what his costs of production were. He didn't know. He turned to Sally in bewilderment. She didn't have an answer either. Mrs. Counts said that she would have to teach a special mathematics lesson the next day so Sally and Jamal would know how to compute profit.

3. Discuss the following questions:

    A. If you ever sold lemonade or some other item, did you make a profit? *Answers will vary.*

    B. Do you know what Mrs. Counts meant by costs of production? *Answers will vary but should include the cost of materials and advertising, pay for workers and rent.*

    C. Why do people start businesses? *Answers will vary and include making money, being their own boss, setting their own hours.*

4. Remind the students that today's lesson is about operating a bookmark business. In the process, they will learn about **costs of production**, **profit** and **revenue**. They will also use their math skills to compute profit or loss.

5. Explain that businesses produce and sell goods and services to earn profit. **Entrepreneurs** and other sellers earn a profit when buyers purchase the products they sell at prices high enough to cover the costs of production. The word entrepreneur comes from a French word, *entreprendre*, which means to undertake something such as starting a business.

6. Divide the class into groups of four to five students to form bookmark companies. Have the students select a name for their company and choose someone in the group to be the entrepreneur and owner.

7. Distribute a bag of resources, a blank piece of paper and a copy of Activities 6.2 and 6.3 to each group. Explain that the bag contains resources that the group should use to produce a sample bookmark. The group does not have to use all the resources in the bag. Allow the groups to look at their resources and brainstorm an idea for a bookmark.

8. Explain that Activity 6.2 is their resource price list. It shows the price the groups must pay for each resource in the bag, as well as the price they must pay for each worker and the rent they must pay for their space.

9. Refer the students to Activity 6.3 and explain that each group must record on this table the costs of producing its sample bookmark, or its unit **costs of production**. Costs of production are the costs of all resources a business uses in producing goods or services. Tell the groups that you will help them figure out their unit costs of production, and each group should choose one person to serve as a recorder.

10. Display Visual 6.1 and demonstrate how to complete the table.

    • Tell the students that businesses must pay for space. Write "Rent" in the first row of Column 1 on the visual, and tell the students to write the word on Activity 6.3. Ask the students how much they must pay for space, based on their Bookmark Resources Price List. *$0.25* Write "$0.25" in the first row of Column 2 on the visual, and tell the group recorders to do the same on their activity. Because each group needs only one space, tell the group recorders to write "1" in the first row of Column 3 on the activity as you write "1" on the visual. Then ask the students what they should write in the first row of Column 4. *$0.25 ($0.25 x 1)* Write "$0.25" on the visual and tell the group recorders to do the same on the activity.

    • Explain that businesses must also pay for **labor**, or all the workers in the group except the entrepreneur. The entrepreneur will earn the profit or have the loss from the company's operations. Tell the group recorders to write "Labor" in the second row of Column 1 while you write the word on the visual. Ask the students how much they must pay each worker. *$0.10* Write "$0.10" on the visual in the second row of Column 2, and ask the group recorders to do the same on the activity. Tell the students to count the number of workers in their group, minus the entrepreneur, and write the number in the second row of Column 3, while you write on the visual the number of workers in one of the student groups. Ask the students what they should write in the second row of Column 4. *The number of students in their group minus 1, the entrepreneur, x $0.10* Tell the recorders to write their groups' labor costs on the activity while you write the labor costs for your sample group on the visual.

- Tell the groups they must pay for each resource they use from their bag. For example, if they use paper for their bookmark, they must list paper on Activity 6.3, along with the cost of paper, the number of pieces of paper they use and their total paper cost. (They do not have to pay for the blank sheet of paper you gave them.)

- Each group should calculate its unit costs of production for its sample bookmark and record the total in the last row of Column 4 on the table.

- The groups may not use any resources other than those in the bag.

11. Tell the students they will have 20 minutes to design their bookmark, calculate their unit costs, produce one sample bookmark their company can sell for $3.00 and develop a slogan that encourages others to buy their bookmark. Tell them to write their slogan on the blank piece of paper.

12. Allow time for the students to work. When they are finished, have each company display its bookmark and slogan on a table or on desks along one side of the classroom.

13. Tell the students that when they were working in their group businesses, they were producers. Now each student will have the opportunity to be a consumer. Give each student three of the $1.00 bills made from Activity 6.4. Tell the students that each bookmark costs $3.00. They will be able to "buy" the bookmark they prefer, but they may not buy their own group's bookmark.

14. Display Visual 6.2. Record each company name on the visual, and ask each entrepreneur to speak for his or her company and "sell" its bookmark:
    - State the company name.
    - Show its bookmark and present the slogan.
    - Ask for a show of hands from the students who want to purchase the bookmark.
    - Record this number on the visual. Ask the entrepreneur to collect $3 from each student who bought the bookmark, and place the money in front of the bookmark on the table or desk where it is displayed. (**Note:** This ensures that each student buys only one bookmark. Later, it will enable the students to count the money to verify their computation of total revenue.)

15. Distribute a copy of Activity 6.5 to each student. Explain that **total revenue** is the quantity of a product sold multiplied by the price of the product. This is the total amount the business receives for selling the product. Tell the students to work in their company groups to answer Questions 2 and 3. Refer the groups to Visual 6.2 for the number of bookmarks their company sold. Tell each group to compute its total revenue by multiplying the quantity sold by the price. Give each group the money its entrepreneur placed in front of its bookmark. Have the groups count the money to verify their calculations of total revenue.

16. Tell the groups to assume that they can produce all the bookmarks they "sold" for the same cost they calculated in Activity

6.3 for one bookmark. Tell them to record this amount in the space under "Unit Cost" in Question 4 of Activity 6.5. Then ask them to calculate their group's total costs by multiplying their unit cost by the number of bookmarks (units) they sold. When the groups have completed Questions 1 through 4 and recorded their calculation on Activity 6.5, collect the papers and record the groups' totals on Visual 6.2.

PART 2

17. Distribute Activity 6.5 to each group and review the previous activities. Remind the students that they determined the total costs and total revenue for their bookmark production. Write the symbols for greater than (>), less than (<) and equal to (=) on the board. Review the symbols with the following questions:
    A. What does the symbol > mean? *Greater than*
    B. What does the symbol < mean? *Less than*
    C. What does the symbol = mean? *Equal to*

18. Write "7 days in a week = 5 weekdays + 2 weekend days" on the board. Explain that this mathematical statement is an **equality**. In an equality, the amount on one side of the equal sign is the same as the amount on the other side of the equal sign. The statement is in balance.

19. Write "5 =" on the board. Ask the students to provide numbers on the other side of the equal sign that would make the statement balance — that is, make it an equality. *4 + 1, 5 + 0, 3 + 2* Ask the students for other examples of equalities. *Answers will vary.*

20. Write "5 < 3 + 3" on the board. Explain that this statement is an **inequality**. The "pointed" end of the symbol for less than points toward the smaller value. In an inequality, the two sides of the statement

are not in balance. They are not equal. In this inequality, 5 is less than 6 so the two sides do not balance.

21. Write "5 > 2 + 2" on the board, and ask a student to read the statement. *The open end of the symbol is facing the larger value.* Ask another student if the two sides are equal (in balance) or unequal (not in balance). *Not in balance.* Ask the students for other examples of inequalities. *Answers will vary but should be unequal, thus an inequality.*

22. Use the following review questions to check the students' understanding of equal to, greater than and less than.
    A. Is the number of vowels in the alphabet less than, greater than or equal to the number of consonants in the alphabet? *Less than*
    B. How would you write the statement 6 is less than 26? (6 < 26) Is this an equality or inequality? Why? *Inequality because the two sides are not equal*
    C. Is the number of players allowed on the field for a soccer team less than, greater than or equal to the number of players allowed on the court for a basketball team? *Greater than*
    D. How would you write the statement 11 is greater than 5? *11 > 5* Is this an equality or an inequality? Why? *Inequality because the two sides are not equal*
    E. On a checker board, is the number of red checker pieces less than, greater than or equal to the number of black checker pieces? *Equal to*
    F. How would you write the statement 12 is equal to 12? *12 = 12* Is this an equality or an inequality? Why? *Equality because both sides are equal*
    G. Is the number of boys in the class less than, greater than or equal to the number of girls in the class? *Answers will vary.* How would you write the answer to this question as a mathematical statement? *Answers will vary.* Is this an equality or an inequality? Why? *Answers*

will vary.

H. How would you write the inequality 5 is greater than 3? *5 > 3*

I. How would you write the inequality 5 is less than 8? *5 < 8*

23. Remind the students that **profit** is the difference between the total revenue a business receives and the total costs it pays for resources. A business earns a profit when its total revenue is greater than its total costs. Entrepreneurs — people who take risks to develop new products or services and start new businesses — must earn a profit, or their business will eventually fail. Profit is income for entrepreneurs and is an **incentive** that encourages them to risk their money and resources. Write the following statement on the board:

Profit occurs when Total Revenue > Total Costs

Profit = Total Revenue – Total Costs

This calculated number can be positive or negative. When it is a positive number, it is called a profit.

24. Explain that when the total costs of a business are greater than its total revenue, the firm has a **loss**. When entrepreneurs start businesses, they face the risk that they will have a loss instead of earning a profit. Write the following statement on the board:

Loss occurs when Total Revenue < Total Costs

Loss = Total Revenue – Total Costs

When this calculated number is negative, it is called a loss.

25. Tell each group to answer Question 5 on Activity 6.5, and then answer Question 6 or 7 and 8, computing its profit or loss for its bookmark company.

26. Display Visual 6.2 again. Have each entrepreneur report his or her company's total revenue, total costs and profit or loss. Record the information on the visual. Discuss the following questions:

A. Which company made the most profit? Why? *The answer will depend on the groups' results, but the reason this company made the most profit was that its costs of production were the lowest and/or many people wanted to buy its bookmark.*

B. If any companies had a loss, why do you think this occurred? *Their costs of production were high and/or not many people wanted to buy their bookmark.*

27. Remind the groups of the statement for profit:

Profit = Total Revenue – Total Costs

Tell them to assume that the same number of people want to buy their bookmarks, but the price has changed. Ask the following questions:

A. If the price of a bookmark were $4 and your unit costs for producing bookmarks were the same as before, what would happen to your group's profit or loss? Why? *If the group had a profit before, its profit would increase because total revenue would increase and total costs would remain the same. If the group had a loss before, its loss would be smaller or it might now make a profit.*

B. If the price of a bookmark remained $3 and your costs increased, what would happen to your group's profit or loss? Why? *If the group had a profit before, its profit would decrease or it might now have a loss because total revenue would remain the same and total costs would increase. If the group had a loss before, it would have a greater loss now.*

C. If a business spent $4.15 to produce a bookmark and could sell the bookmark for $3.00, would the business have a profit or a loss? Why? *A loss because costs were greater than revenue*

CLOSURE

28. Ask the groups to work on the following review questions. Each group may work on all the questions, or you may assign each group a question to answer and report to the class.

    A. What is an equation? *The amount on one side of the equal sign is the same as the amount on the other side of the equal sign. The two sides are in balance.*

    B. What is an inequality? *The two sides of the statement are not in balance and are not equal.*

    C. What are total costs? *The costs of all resources a producer uses to make a good or provide a service*

    D. What is total revenue? *The amount a business receives from the sale of its goods or services*

    E. What is profit? *Profit is total revenue minus total costs.*

    F. What is an entrepreneur? *A person who takes risks to start new businesses and develop new products or services*

    G. What must a business do to earn a profit and avoid a loss? *Keep costs low and sell the product at a price greater than its unit cost.*

    H. Why must a business make careful decisions about which resources to buy? *Resources cost money and costs affect profits.*

    I. What would happen to a business if no one wanted to buy its products? *It will have losses and eventually fail.*

    J. Why is profit important to entrepreneurs? *It determines whether the entrepreneur can continue in business, it provides the entrepreneur with a monetary reward and it serves as an incentive for entrepreneurs to accept the risks of starting and running a business.*

ASSESSMENT

Distribute a copy of Activity 6.6 to each student. Review the instructions and allow time for the students to complete their work or assign the activity as homework. Go over the answers with the students.

1. What were Jamal and Sally's total costs? Show your work. *$3.50 + $1.00 +$0.75 + $0.75 = $6.00*

2. Write the equation for Jamal and Sally's total revenue. *Total Revenue = Price x Quantity Sold* What was their total revenue? *$0.25 x 60 = $15.00*

3. Was Jamal and Sally's total revenue < or > their total costs? *> because their total revenue of $15 was greater than their total costs of $6*

4. Who are the entrepreneurs in this activity? Why? *Jamal and Sally, because they risk their resources and time to sell lemonade*

5. Did Jamal and Sally earn a profit or have a loss? How much was their profit or loss? *They earned a profit of $9 because $15 – $6 = $9.*

6. If Jamal and Sally's total costs were $16.50, would they earn a profit or have a loss? How much would their profit or loss be? *They would have a loss of $1.50 because $15 – $16.50 = – $1.50.*

VISUAL 6.1
COMPUTING UNIT COSTS OF PRODUCTION

Company Name: ____

In Column 1, list each resource you used to produce your sample bookmark.

In Column 2, write the price for each resource, using the Bookmark Resource Price List on Activity 6.2.

In Column 3, write the number of units of each resource that your company used. (For labor, write the number of students in your group, minus the entrepreneur.)

In Column 4, compute the cost of each resource by multiplying the number in Column 2 by the number in Column 3.

Add the amounts in Column 4 to find the unit costs of producing a bookmark. **Write your unit costs** (total costs of production for one bookmark) in the bottom row of Column 4.

1	2	3	4
Resource	Resource Price per Unit	Number of Units Used	Total Resource Cost (Column 2 x Column 3)
	Total Costs of Production for One Bookmark		

VISUAL 6.2
BOOKMARKS BY THE NUMBERS

1	2	3	4	5
Bookmark Company Name	**Quantity of Bookmarks Sold**	**Total Revenue**	**Total Cost**	**Profit / Loss**

ACTIVITY 6.1
MONEY MATTERS REVIEW

Directions: Calculate the answers to these questions. Show your work.

A. Suppose you have been saving your money to buy a new bicycle. The price of the bicycle is $175.50. You have saved $75.25. How much more money must you save?

B. You can walk the neighbor's dog for three days. She will pay you $3.00 a day. If you take the job, how much money will you earn? If you put all of your earnings in your savings account, how much will you still need to buy the bike?

C. Your sister is selling lemonade. The price is $0.15 a cup. If she sells four cups, how much money will she have?

D. You bought candy at a store. You paid $0.15 for gooey worms, $0.20 for jelly beans and $0.07 for sour stars. What is the total you spent? If you paid with a $1.00 bill, how much change will you receive?

ACTIVITY 6.2
BOOKMARK RESOURCE PRICE LIST

Resource	Price
Space (rent)	$0.25
Worker (wage)	$0.10

ACTIVITY 6.3
COMPUTING UNIT COSTS OF PRODUCTION

Company Name: ____

In Column 1, list each resource you used to produce your sample bookmark.

In Column 2, write the price for each resource, using the Bookmark Resource Price List on Activity 6.2.

In Column 3, write the number of units of each resource that your company used. (For labor, write the number of students in your group, minus the entrepreneur.)

In Column 4, compute the cost of each resource by multiplying the number in Column 2 by the number in Column 3.

Add the amounts in Column 4 to find the unit costs of producing a bookmark. **Write your unit costs** (total costs of production for one bookmark) in the bottom row of Column 4.

1 Resource	2 Resource Price per Unit	3 Number of Units Used	4 Total Resource Cost (Column 2 x Column 3)
	Total Costs of Production for One Bookmark		

ACTIVITY 6.4
DOLLARS FOR BOOKMARKS

$1 ONE DOLLAR $1 **E** $1 ENTREPRENEUR $1	$1 ONE DOLLAR $1 **E** $1 ENTREPRENEUR $1
$1 ONE DOLLAR $1 **E** $1 ENTREPRENEUR $1	$1 ONE DOLLAR $1 **E** $1 ENTREPRENEUR $1
$1 ONE DOLLAR $1 **E** $1 ENTREPRENEUR $1	$1 ONE DOLLAR $1 **E** $1 ENTREPRENEUR $1
$1 ONE DOLLAR $1 **E** $1 ENTREPRENEUR $1	$1 ONE DOLLAR $1 **E** $1 ENTREPRENEUR $1

ACTIVITY 6.5
COMPUTING BOOKMARK PROFITS

Company Name:	Entrepreneur:

1. The selling price of your company's bookmark is	**$3.00**

2. How many bookmarks did you sell?	

3. Use this equation to determine your company's total revenue:

Selling Price	**x**	**Quantity Sold**	**=**	**Total Revenue**
	x		**=**	

4. Use this equation to determine your company's total cost:

Unit Cost	**x**	**Quantity Produced**	**=**	**Total Cost**
	x		**=**	

5. Is your company's total revenue > (greater than) its total cost
or is your company's total revenue < (less than) its total cost?

6. If your company's total revenue was greater than its total cost,
use this equation to determine your company's profit:

Profit	**=**	**Total Revenue**	**–**	**Total Cost**
	=		**–**	

7. If your total cost was greater than your total revenue,
use this equation to determine your company's loss.

Loss	**=**	**Total Revenue**	**–**	**Total Cost**
	=		**–**	

8. Did your company's entrepreneur earn income (profit)?

ACTIVITY 6.6
ASSESSMENT: LUSCIOUS LEMONADE

Directions: Read the paragraph below. Help Jamal and Sally use this information to figure out whether their lemonade business earned a profit or had a loss. Show your work. (Use the back if you need more room.)

Mrs. Counts talked with Jamal and Sally about their lemonade stand. She learned that they sold 60 cups of lemonade at $0.25 each. She also learned that Jamal's mother charged them for the resources they used to make the lemonade:
- $3.50 for lemonade mix
- $1.00 to rent the table for the lemonade stand
- $0.75 for cups
- $0.75 to rent the pitcher, spoon and measuring cup

1. What were Jamal and Sally's total costs? Show your work.

2. Write the equation for Jamal and Sally's total revenue. What was their total revenue?

3. Was Jamal and Sally's total revenue < or > their total costs?

4. Who are the entrepreneurs in this activity? Why?

5. Did Jamal and Sally earn a profit or have a loss? How much was their profit or loss?

6. If Jamal and Sally's total costs were $16.50, would they earn a profit or have a loss? How much would their profit or loss be?

Lesson 7 - Go Fly a Kite

OVERVIEW

This lesson focuses on resources and barter (economics) and geometry (mathematics). After reviewing the concept of bartering, the students roll a four-sided dice to gather some of the resources they will need to build a tetrahedron kite, which is based on the shape of a platonic solid. Then they barter to get the rest of the materials they will need. During this process, the students identify the characteristics of intermediate goods and use these goods to build their kite.

CONCEPTS

Economics
> Barter
> Intermediate goods
> Productive resources (natural resources, capital goods and human resources)
> Trade

Mathematics
> Equilateral
> Geometry as related to two- and three-dimensional shapes
> Metric measurement
> Platonic solids
> Tetrahedron
> Vertex

CONTENT STANDARDS

Economics
Standard 1
> • **Benchmark 9 for 4th grade:** Productive resources are the natural resources, human resources and capital goods available to make goods and services.
> • **Benchmark 10 for 4th grade:** Natural resources, such as land, are "gifts of nature"; they are present without human intervention.
> • **Benchmark 11 for 4th grade:** Human resources are the quantity and quality of human effort directed toward producing goods and services.
> • **Benchmark 12 for 4th grade:** Capital goods are goods produced and used to make other goods and services.

Standard 5
> • **Benchmark 2 for 4th grade:** The oldest form of exchange is barter - the direct trading of goods and services between people.
> • **Benchmark 3 for 4th grade:** People voluntarily exchange goods and services because they expect to be better off after the exchange.

Mathematics
Geometry
> • Analyze characteristics and properties of two- and three-dimensional geometric shapes and develop mathematical arguments about geometric relationships.
> • Use visualization, spatial reasoning and geometric modeling to solve problems.

Connections
> • Recognize and apply mathematics in contexts outside of mathematics

OBJECTIVES

The students will:
1. Identify attributes of two- and three-dimensional shapes.

2. Identify and build a 3-D object from a 2-D representation of the object.

3. Identify productive resources.

4. Describe bartering as the exchange of goods and services for other goods and services without the use of money.

TIME REQUIRED

120 minutes

MATERIALS

(**Note:** This activity requires advance preparation. You will need to make a sample tetrahedron dice and tetrahedron kite, cut Activity 7.4 into tickets, collect enough materials for each team to construct one kite (it's important not to provide extra materials) and divide the materials into sets that you will distribute during a game the students play using the tetrahedron dice. To figure out the number of teams you'll have, divide the number of students in the class by four.)

1. Visuals 7.1 and 7.2

2. One copy of Activity 7.1, 7.2, 7.3 and 7.4 for each team

3. One copy of Activity 7.5 cut into tickets (Mount on stiff cardboard for use with more than one class. If you have more than eight groups, you will need to make additional copies of this page.)

4. One copy of Activity 7.6 for each student

5. Materials for each team to make one kite:
   • 24 stiff plastic straws
   • 9 meters of string (not yarn)
   • 4 sheets of colored tissue paper
   • One pair of scissors and one pencil for each student
   • One meter stick for each team
   • Tape and glue for each team
   • **Optional:** One spool of kite string for each kite

ADDITIONAL RESOURCES

For additional curriculum connections, Web links, technology applications and suggested children's literature that will help you teach this lesson, go to
http://mathandecon.ncee.net/35/lesson7

PROCEDURE

1. Begin this lesson by demonstrating a **barter** situation, but don't use the word "barter" to describe the demonstration. Think of a small item that some, but not all, the students might have, such as a red marker. Ask if anyone who has this item would be willing to exchange it for some other small item. Ask the students individually until one agrees to the exchange. Try to start with a student who probably does not have a red marker so you can ask several people. After the exchange, ask the students if they know the name of the activity they just witnessed. ***Bartering: exchanging goods or services for other goods or services directly without exchanging money***

2. Discuss other bartering experiences the students or their friends and families have had, such as exchanging toys, trading clothes or books, baby-sitting in exchange for haircutting, making a home repair for legal services, doing a paper route for mowing a lawn. Ask the students if bartering is a good thing to do. ***Answers will vary and may include that it is usually easy to barter if both parties want the items offered.***

3. Tell the students they will participate in an activity that combines bartering with constructing a special kite using a three-dimensional shape. Review some of the basic three-dimensional shapes and ask the students to give real-world examples of each. ***Answers will vary and include***
   • ***sphere: ball***
   • ***cylinder: soft-drink can***
   • ***rectangular prism: tissue box***
   • ***cone: party hat***

- *cube: ice cube*
- *pyramid: Egyptian pyramids*

4. Show the students a completed tetrahedron kite. Explain that these kites are special because they are made by putting four **tetrahedrons** together.

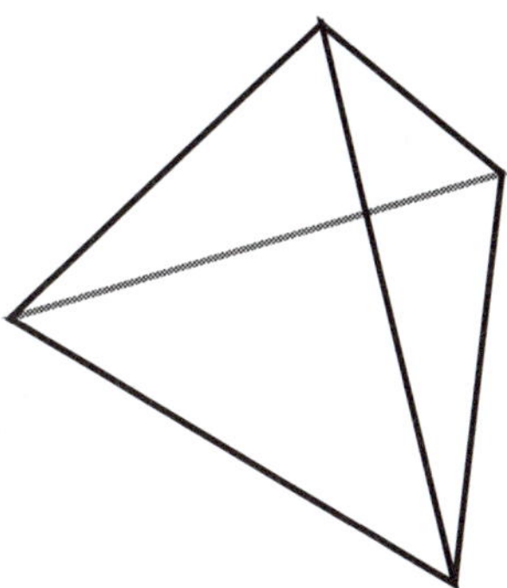

A tetrahedron is a three-dimensional shape made up of four equilateral triangles with the same number of edges meeting at each vertex. It is one of the five **platonic solids**. A platonic solid is a three-dimensional shape that uses the same regular polygon, or two-dimensional equilateral shape, for every face and has the same number of faces meeting at each vertex. Only five platonic solids are possible, and the tetrahedron is the one with the fewest sides: four.

5. Tell the students that before they can make their tetrahedron kites, they must collect the necessary **productive resources**. Explain that there are three types of productive resources:
   - Natural resources — "gifts of nature" present without human intervention
   - Human resources — quality and quantity of human effort directed toward producing goods and services
   - Capital goods (resources) — goods people produce and use to make other goods and services
   Ask the students for examples of each type of resource.
   Answers will vary and may include
   - *natural resources: sunlight, soil, trees, coal*
   - *human resources: teachers, mechanics, doctors, salespeople*
   - *capital goods: hammers, computers, school buses, overhead projectors*

6. Ask the students which resource they provide with their labor. *Human*

7. Tell the students they will also need some **capital goods**. Explain that capital goods are goods such as scissors, hammers and paint brushes that people use to make other goods. Tell the students that they will also need **intermediate goods**, which are materials such as glue and paint that are used up in production and become part of the final good. Ask the students to think of other intermediate goods they use at school. *Answers will vary and include construction paper, pencil lead and clay.*

8. Give each student a copy of Activity 7.1, and tell them these are the instructions for making a tetrahedron kite. Go over the instructions with the students and ask them to underline or highlight all the items they will need. Show them Activity 7.2 so they know what a gore pattern is. *They will need 24 stiff straws, nine meters of string, four sheets of tissue paper, one gore pattern, a meter stick, scissors, glue and a tetrahedron dice.*

9. Display Visual 7.1 but hide the "Labor" column. Have volunteers call out the items they underlined, and ask the class whether each is an intermediate good or a capital good. Write the items on the visual in the appropriate column. *Materials or intermediate goods: tissue paper, straws, string and glue. Capital goods: scissors, gore pattern, pencil and meter stick*

10. Remind the students that they will need another resource to make their kite: the human resource, or their labor. Ask them to look over the directions again and identify which tasks they will be doing

as they construct their kite. Uncover the "Labor" column on Visual 7.1 and list their answers in this column. ***Rolling dice, cutting tissue paper, tying string, measuring string, threading straws, cutting string, gluing tissue paper***

11. Tell the students that they are going to play a game called "Tetra Trades" to collect the intermediate goods they will need to make their kite. Arrange the students in teams of four. There can be teams with fewer than four students if needed, but no teams should have more than four. Have the students sit together to work because this activity takes group discussion.

12. Give each team a copy of Activity 7.3 and show the class the sample paper tetrahedron dice. Tell the students they will make their own paper tetrahedron dice and use it to "roll" for the intermediate goods they will need to construct their kite.

13. Give each team scissors and tape. Have them carefully cut out their dice and fold and tape the sides together to form the tetrahedron. Ask the following questions:
    A. How many faces does a tetrahedron have? ***Four: A face is the two-dimensional shape that forms the flat surface on each side of the tetrahedron.***
    B. What shape are all the faces? ***Triangles***
    C. How many edges does the tetrahedron have? ***Six: An edge is where two faces meet.***
    D. How many vertices does it have? ***Four: A vertex is where three or more edges meet.***

14. Explain that each team will roll its tetrahedron dice four times to get the kite materials: one roll for each team member. Tell the students that if a team has fewer than four members, some students will roll the dice more than once. Roll the sample dice and show the students that they will get the intermediate good pictured on the bottom of the tetrahedron. For exam-

ple, if a picture of straws is on the bottom, you will give them a ticket that represents 24 straws (six straws for each tetrahedron, four tetrahedrons to make a kite, so 6 x 4 = 24). Tell the students that they may roll the same intermediate good more than once, so they may get more than one ticket for this good. Ask them how they could solve this problem. ***They could trade, or barter, their extra tickets for the tickets they need. You may have to help them with this answer.*** Tell them that they will have a chance to barter; and when all the teams have a ticket for each good, you will give them the materials and they will make their kites.

15. Give each team one copy of Activity 7.4, and tell them to record the intermediate good they get each time they roll the dice. After each roll, they should send one team member to you to collect the appropriate ticket made from Activity 7.5.
    (**Note:** If you run out of tickets for one intermediate good, tell the team to roll again until it gets a good for which you still have tickets.)

16. Display Visual 7.2 and ask if any team has a ticket for each of the four intermediate goods it needs to make the kite. (**Note:** This would be rare but could happen. Most teams will not have the necessary materials. They will have more of one item and be missing an item.) Record the teams that have the intermediate goods to begin construction. Tell the rest of the teams that they will be allowed to barter with each other for the intermediate goods they need. Have each team appoint a member to bring one extra ticket to the front of the room. Tell the students that they will have one minute to make one trade. At the end of a minute, have the teams reassess whether they now have tickets for all four goods. Record on Visual 7.2 the teams that can make a kite after one trade.

17. Repeat the bartering process until all teams have the correct number of interme-

diate goods to make their kite. Stop, check and record on Visual 7.2 the teams with all the resources after each trade.

18. Ask the students if they see any problems with bartering as a way to get items they need. ***Answers will vary, but the students should realize the difficulty of finding someone who has the goods they need. Bartering has a cost in human resources because it takes time to find someone willing to make a trade.***

19. Have the teams send a member to you to turn in their tickets and receive their intermediate goods.
(**Note:** Depending on the length of your class period, you may want to hand out the materials and have the students make their kites on the following day. If you do this, tell the students to keep their tickets in a safe place until the next class.)

20. Display the completed tetrahedron kite model, and review the instructions on Activity 7.1 with the students. Tell them that it is important for them to follow the instructions exactly if they want to build their kites successfully. Allow the teams to work independently while you circulate to assist them, or the class can work through the instructions step-by-step as you model each step.
Optional: Another way to complete the kites is to have the teams make the four tetrahedrons independently and then have them work with you on tying the tetrahedrons together to form the kite.
Optional: The students can make a bigger kite by treating four kites as four tetrahedrons and assembling them into one kite. Or they can assemble 16 tetrahedron kites to make a very large kite. You might want to tell the students that Alexander Graham Bell, the man who invented the telephone, also invented the tetrahedron kite. One of Bell's kites had more than 3,000 tetrahedrons.

CLOSURE

21. Bring the class back together and display the kites. The students can hang them from the ceiling of the room, or, if the weather permits, fly them outside. Ask the following questions to review the important content of the lesson:
    A. What are the two categories of productive resources you need to produce a tetrahedron kite? ***Labor or human resources to measure, cut, paste and assemble materials and capital goods such as the gore pattern, scissors and meter stick***
    B. Do you feel that bartering was a good method for allocating materials for the kites? ***Answers will vary. Some students might feel that bartering was efficient because everyone eventually got the materials they needed or their team didn't have to barter more than once or twice to obtain the needed materials. Other students may say it was inefficient because they had to make many trades to get all the materials they needed.***
    C. In what circumstances do we barter today to get the things we want? ***Answers will vary and may include bartering with collector cards, toys, school supplies, lunch items, clothing, CDs and books.***

ASSESSMENT

Activity 7.6 reviews the bartering process and basic three-dimensional shapes: cylinder, sphere and rectangular prism. Distribute a copy of the activity to each student. Review the instructions and tell the students to answer Questions 1, 2 and 3. Allow time for the students to finish and go over their answers. Next tell the students to answer the rest of the questions. Again, allow time for them to work and go over their answers.

1. Which three lunch items look like a cylinder? ***Small can of chips, can of root beer and carton of yogurt***

2. Which three items look like a rectangular prism? ***PB&J sandwich, brownie and juice box***

3. Which three items look like a sphere? ***Meatballs, peach and orange***

4. Fill in the blanks below to explain how Luis, Michael and Sonya can barter their lunch items so that they each have a cylinder, a rectangular prism and a sphere.
    A. Luis has two lunch items that are the same shape: ***meatballs*** and a ***peach***. He needs to barter for a ***rectangular prism*** shape, so he barters a ***meatball or peach*** for a ***PB&J sandwich, brownie or juice box***.
    B. Michael has two lunch items that are the same shape: a ***yogurt*** and a ***can of chips***. He needs to barter for a ***rectangular prism*** shape, so he barters a ***yogurt or can of chips*** for a ***PB&J sandwich, brownie or juice box***.
    C. Sonya has three lunch items that are the same shape: a ***PB&J sandwich***, a ***brownie*** and a ***juice box***. She needs to barter for two different shapes: a ***cylinder*** and a ***sphere***. She first barters a ***PB&J sandwich, brownie or juice box*** for a ***yogurt, can of chips or root beer*** and then barters a ***PB&J sandwich, brownie or juice box*** for a ***peach, Italian meatball or orange***.

5. Draw a picture of what each student actually ate for lunch. ***Answers will vary. Each student needs to have a sphere, a cylinder and a rectangular prism.***

VISUAL 7.1
MATERIALS AND PRODUCTIVE RESOURCES
FOR TETRAHEDRON KITES

Materials (intermediate goods)	**Capital Goods**	**Labor** (human resources)

VISUAL 7.2
TETRA TRADES

Identify the four intermediate goods you have following the four rolls of the dice. What goods do you need? How many times did you barter to get the intermediate goods to build your kite? What are the problems with bartering?

	Had all four intermediate goods. **Needed 0 trades**	Had some intermediate goods. **Needed 1 trade**	**Needed 2 trades**	**Needed 3 trades**	**Needed 4 trades**
Team Names					

ACTIVITY 7.1
DIRECTIONS FOR MAKING A TETRAHEDRON KITE

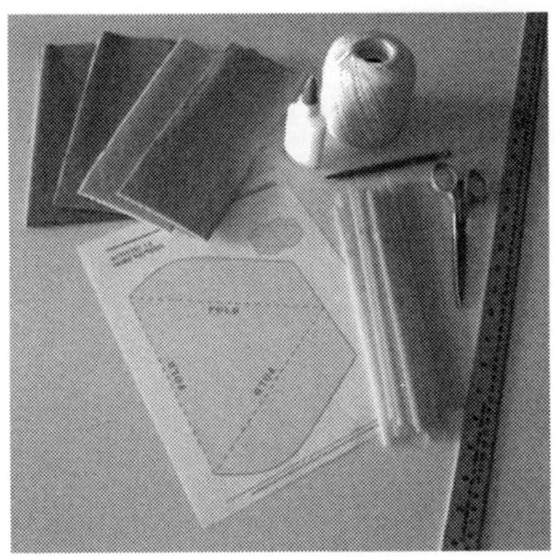

Step 1. You will play a game with a tetrahedron dice to collect some of the materials you need: 24 stiff straws, 9 meters of string, four sheets of tissue paper and one gore pattern. Your teacher will give you a meter stick, scissors, a pencil and glue.

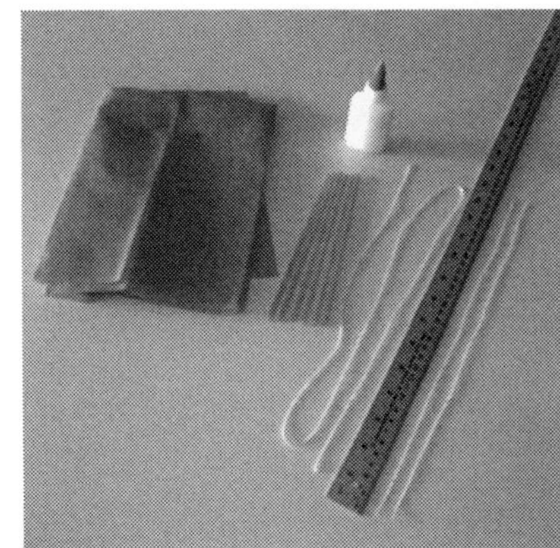

Step 2. After you have the materials, divide them into four groups, one for each tetrahedron frame: one piece of tissue paper, six straws, one piece of string 1 meter long and two pieces of string about 35 centimeters long.

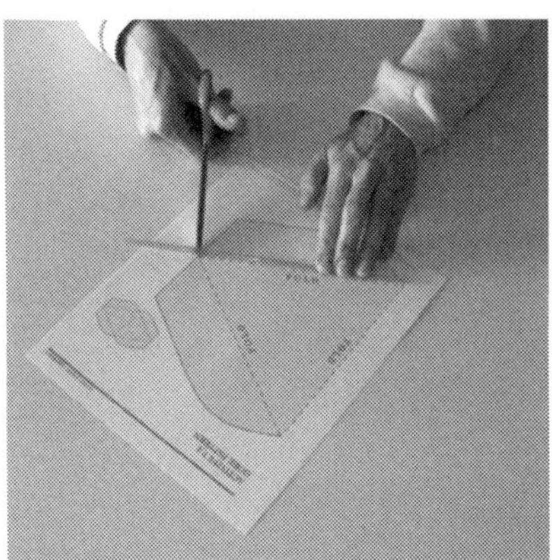

Step 3. Put one straw on one of the dotted lines on the gore pattern (Activity 7.2). Cut the straw to make it the same length as the dotted line. Use the cut straw to measure the other 23 straws, and cut them so that all your straws are the same length.

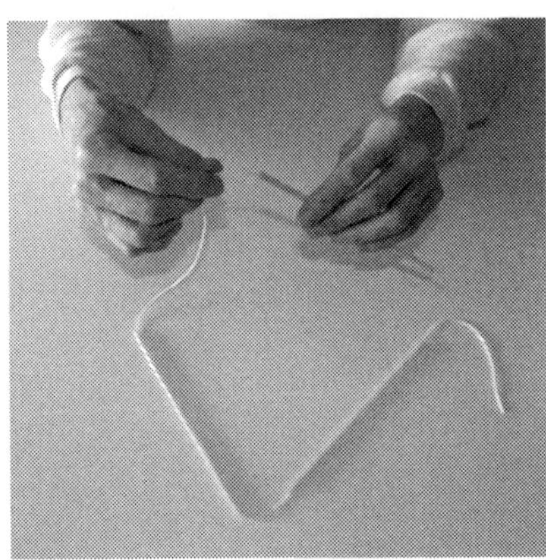

Step 4. Make the four tetrahedron frames by following these steps for each frame: First, thread three straws onto the 1-meter length of string.

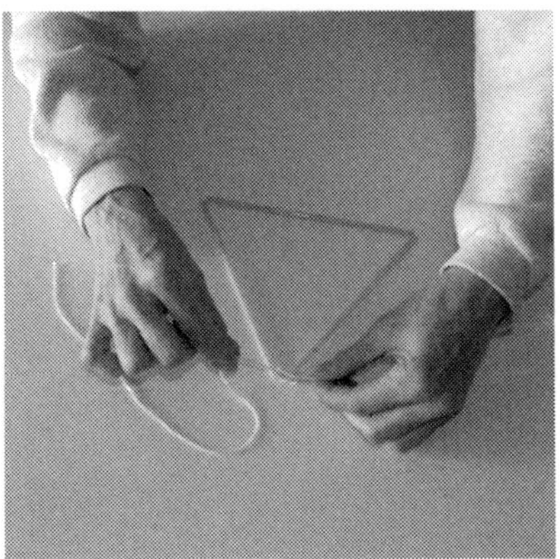

Step 5. Tie the ends of the string together to make a triangle. Each straw will form one side of the triangle. Leave one end of the string longer than the other so you have a "tail" on one corner.

Step 6. Take the two shorter strings and tie one onto each of the corners that does not have a tail. You should now have a tail of longer string on all three corners of the triangle.

ACTIVITY 7.1 (continued)
DIRECTIONS FOR MAKING A TETRAHEDRON KITE

Step 7. Take one of the remaining three straws and thread it onto one of the shorter tails. Take another straw and thread it onto the other short tail. Tie the ends of the tails tightly to form a second triangle.

Step 8. Thread the last straw on the remaining tail. Tie the string tightly to the opposite corner. This will complete your first four-sided, three-dimensional tetrahedron frame. Repeat Steps 4 through 8 to make three more frames.

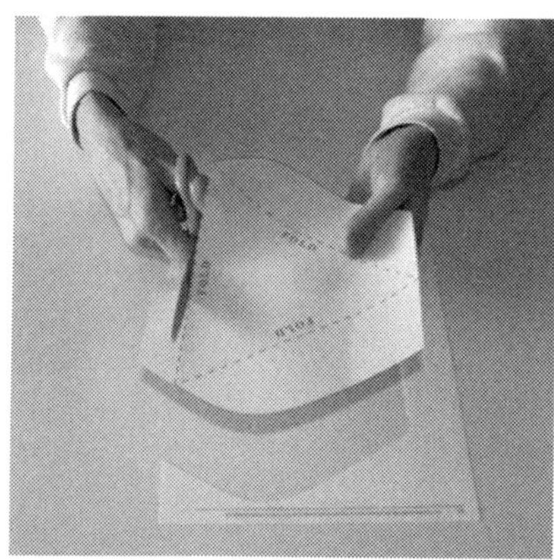

Step 9. Make the tissue paper coverings, or gores, for the frames by following these steps: First, cut out the gore pattern on Activity 7.2.

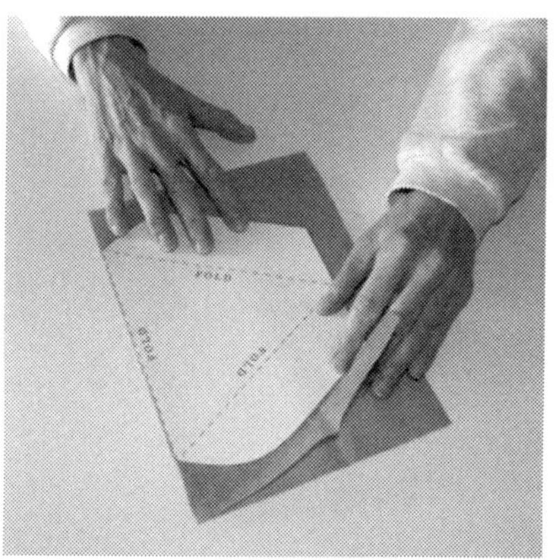

Step 10. Fold a full sheet of tissue paper neatly in half. Place the gore pattern on the folded edge of the tissue paper, with the dotted edge of the pattern on the fold.

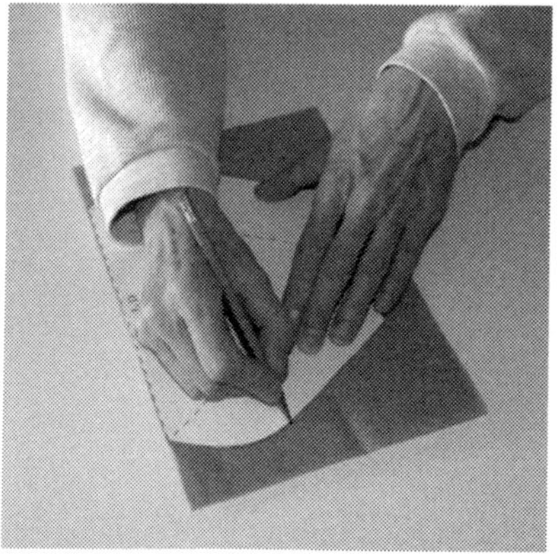

Step 11. Draw lightly around the pattern with the pencil, and carefully cut out the tissue-paper shape. Follow the lines exactly, and do not cut along the fold.

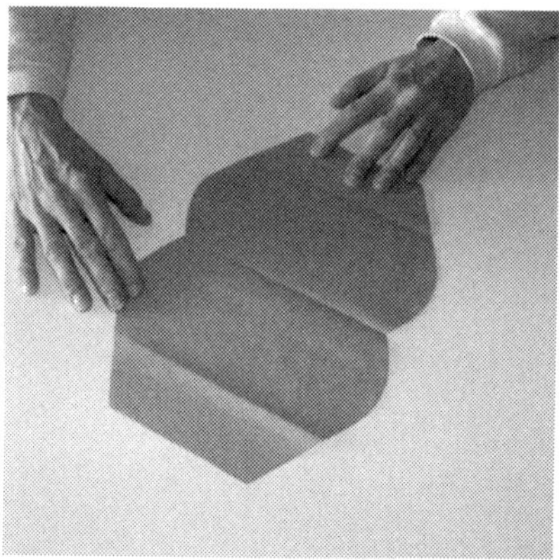

Step 12. Unfold the tissue paper. Use the gore pattern to trace and cut three more pieces of paper to make four gores.

ACTIVITY 7.1 (continued)
DIRECTIONS FOR MAKING A TETRAHEDRON KITE

Step 13. Cover each tetrahedron frame with the tissue-paper gores by following these steps: First, place a very thin line of glue along the fold in the center of one tissue-paper gore.

Step 14. Lay a straw that forms any side of one tetrahedron on the line of glue, holding the rest of the tetrahedron upright. This is easier if two people work together.

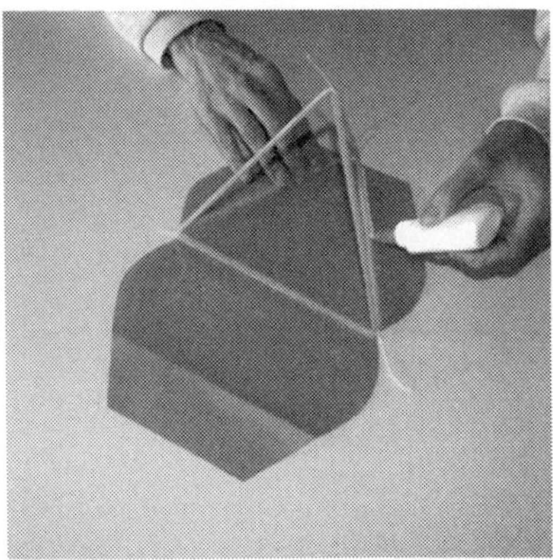

Step 15. Let go of the tetrahedron and let it drop down on one side of the gore. Put a thin line of glue along the outside edge of one of the straws. Also put a thin line of glue around the edge of the flap next to the straw.

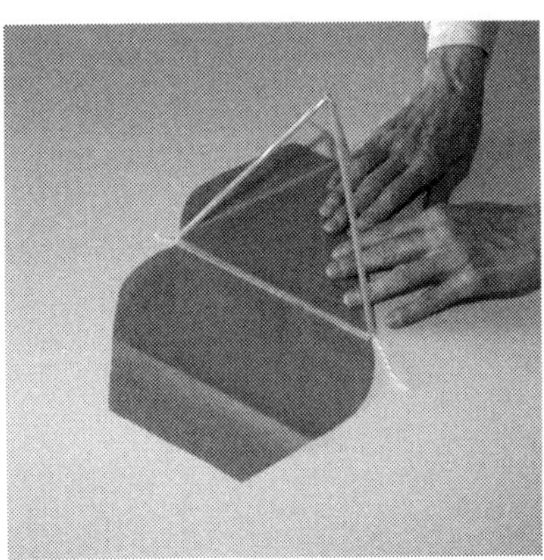

Step 16. Fold the flap with the glue over the straw toward the inside of the triangle and press down.

Step 17. Put a thin line of glue along the outside edge of the other straw and around the edge of the other flap. Fold this flap over the straw toward the inside of the triangle and press down.

Step 18. Roll your tetrahedron to the other side of the tissue-paper gore.

ACTIVITY 7.1 (continued)
DIRECTIONS FOR MAKING A TETRAHEDRON KITE

Step 19. Glue the flaps on this side the same way you glued the flaps on the other side. You should now have a tetrahedron with two covered sides and two open sides.

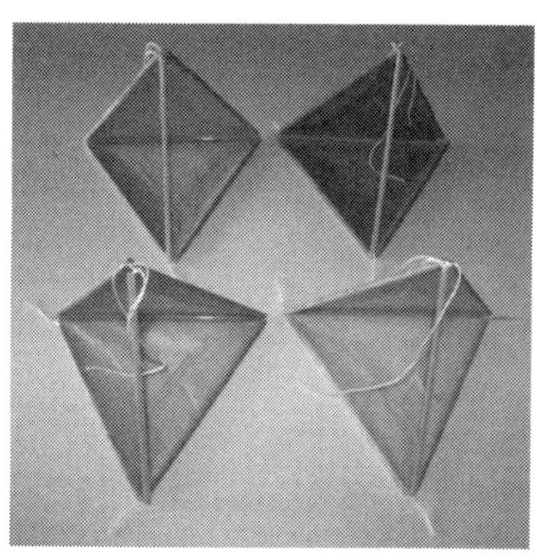

Step 20. Follow Steps 13 through 19 to cover the remaining three tetrahedron frames.

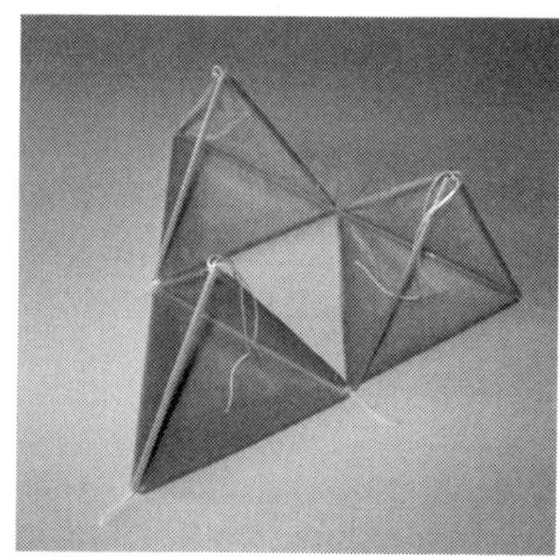

Step 21. Now assemble your kite. First place three of the finished tetrahedrons on the table, with one covered side down, so they form a large triangle shape. Make sure all of the other covered sides are facing in the same direction.

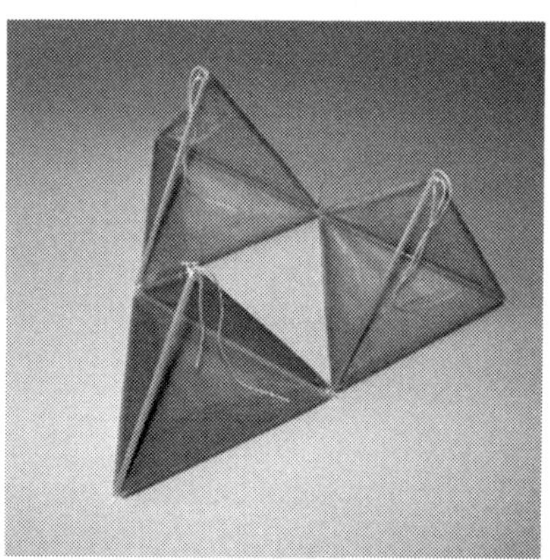

Step 22. Cut three short pieces of string long enough to tie the tetrahedron corners together where they touch. Tie each of the three corners tightly. Trim off the leftover string.

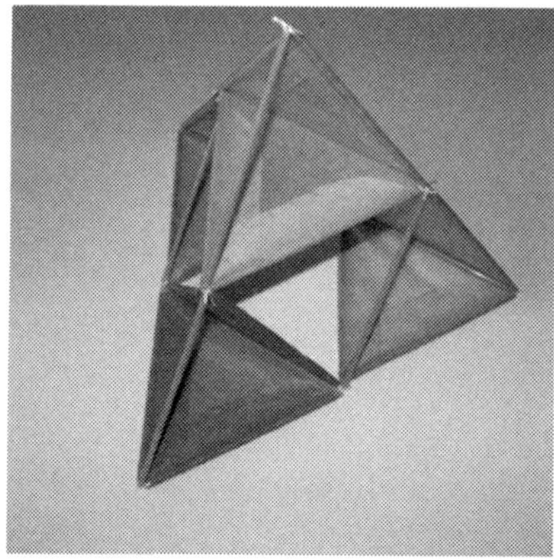

Step 23. Cut three more short pieces of string. Put the fourth tetrahedron on top of the other three. Use the pieces of string to tie the corners tightly together where they touch. Trim off the leftover string. Let the kite dry thoroughly.

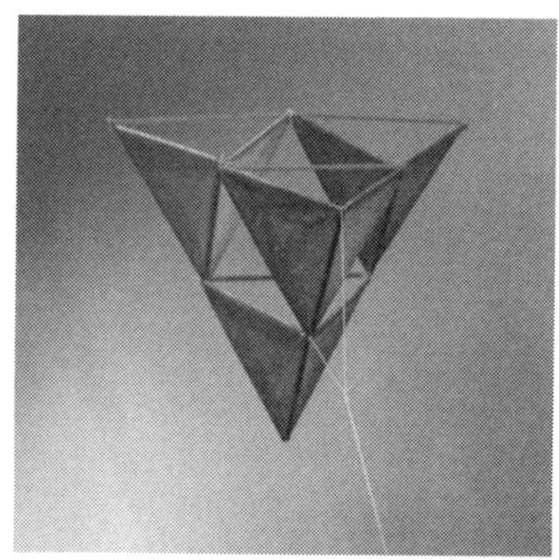

Step 24. Display your kite in class or go outside and fly it! You can also make a bigger kite by tying together four kites the way you tied together the four tetrahedrons.

ACTIVITY 7.2
GORE PATTERN

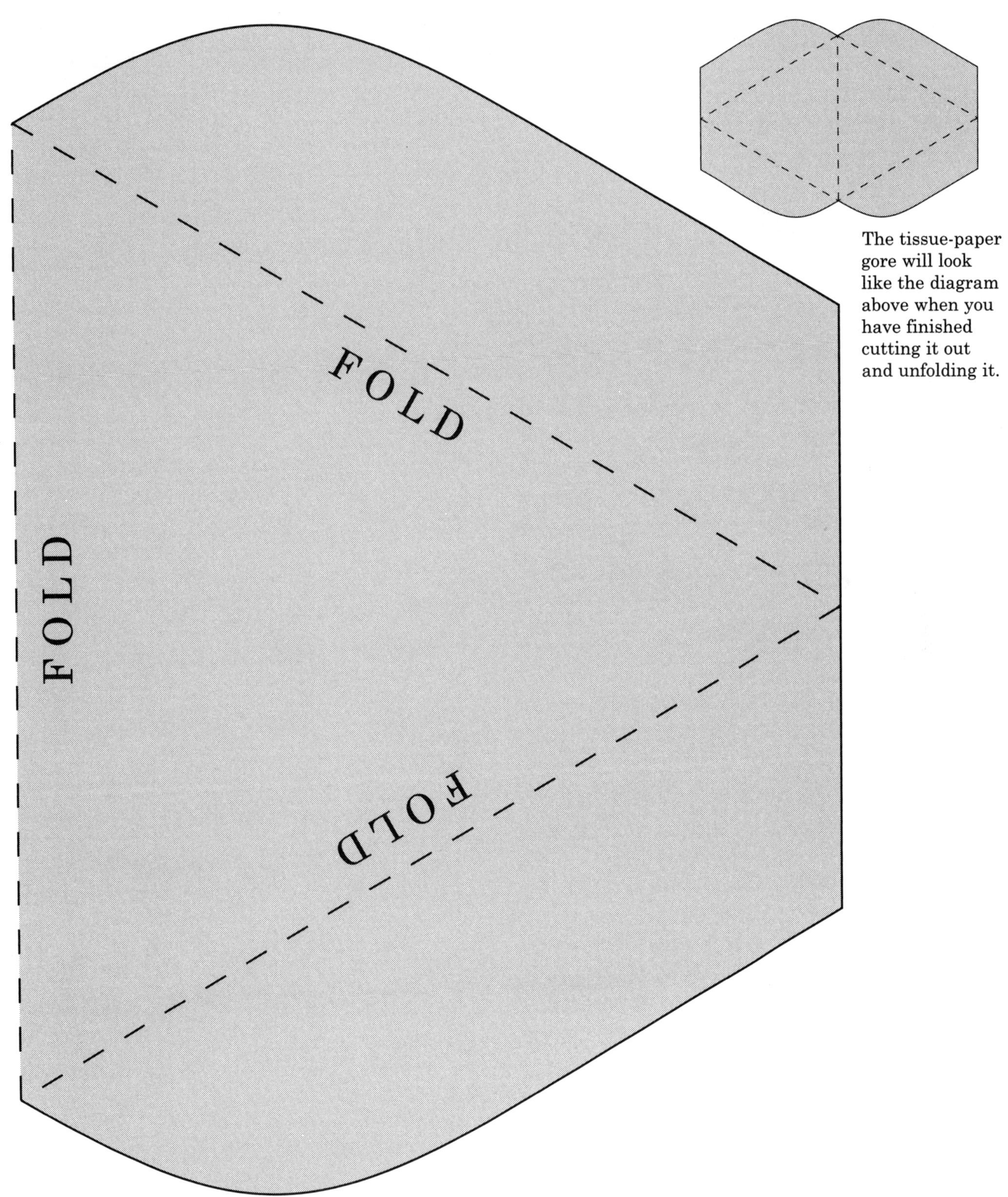

The tissue-paper gore will look like the diagram above when you have finished cutting it out and unfolding it.

ACTIVITY 7.3
TETRAHEDRON DICE

Cut out the tetrahedron and fold on the
dotted lines. Tape the sides together
using the tabs to form a pyramid-
shaped tetrahedron dice.

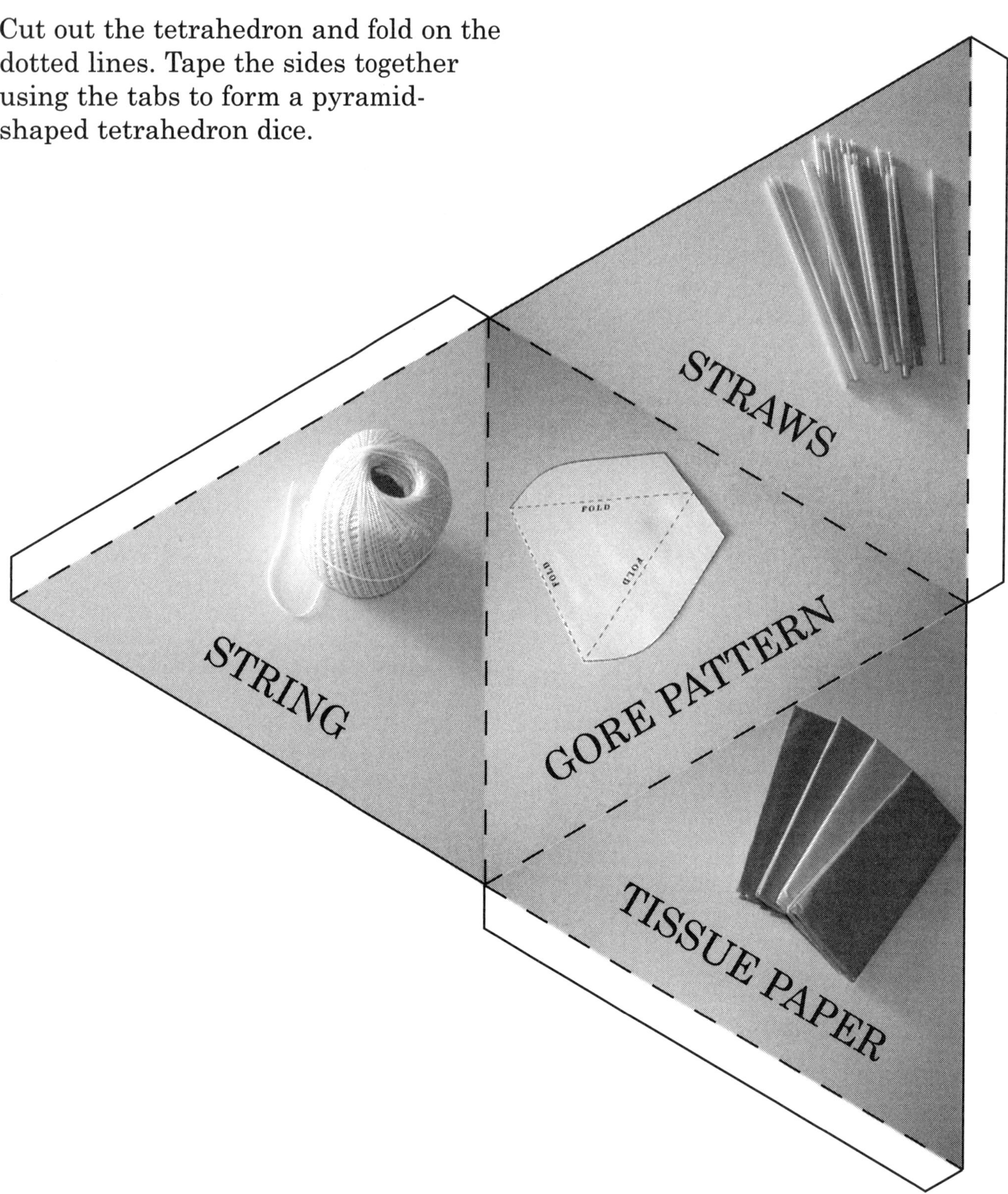

   MATHEMATICS AND ECONOMICS: CONNECTIONS FOR LIFE, © NATIONAL COUNCIL ON ECONOMIC EDUCATION, NEW YORK, N.Y.

ACTIVITY 7.4
GETTING YOUR INTERMEDIATE GOODS

Put an X in the column to indicate which intermediate good your team got each time it rolled the tetrahedron dice.

	Straws	String	Tissue Paper	Gore Pattern
Roll 1				
Roll 2				
Roll 3				
Roll 4				

ACTIVITY 7.5
INTERMEDIATE GOODS TICKETS

24 drinking straws	24 drinking straws
24 drinking straws	24 drinking straws
24 drinking straws	24 drinking straws
24 drinking straws	24 drinking straws

ACTIVITY 7.5 (continued)
INTERMEDIATE GOODS TICKETS

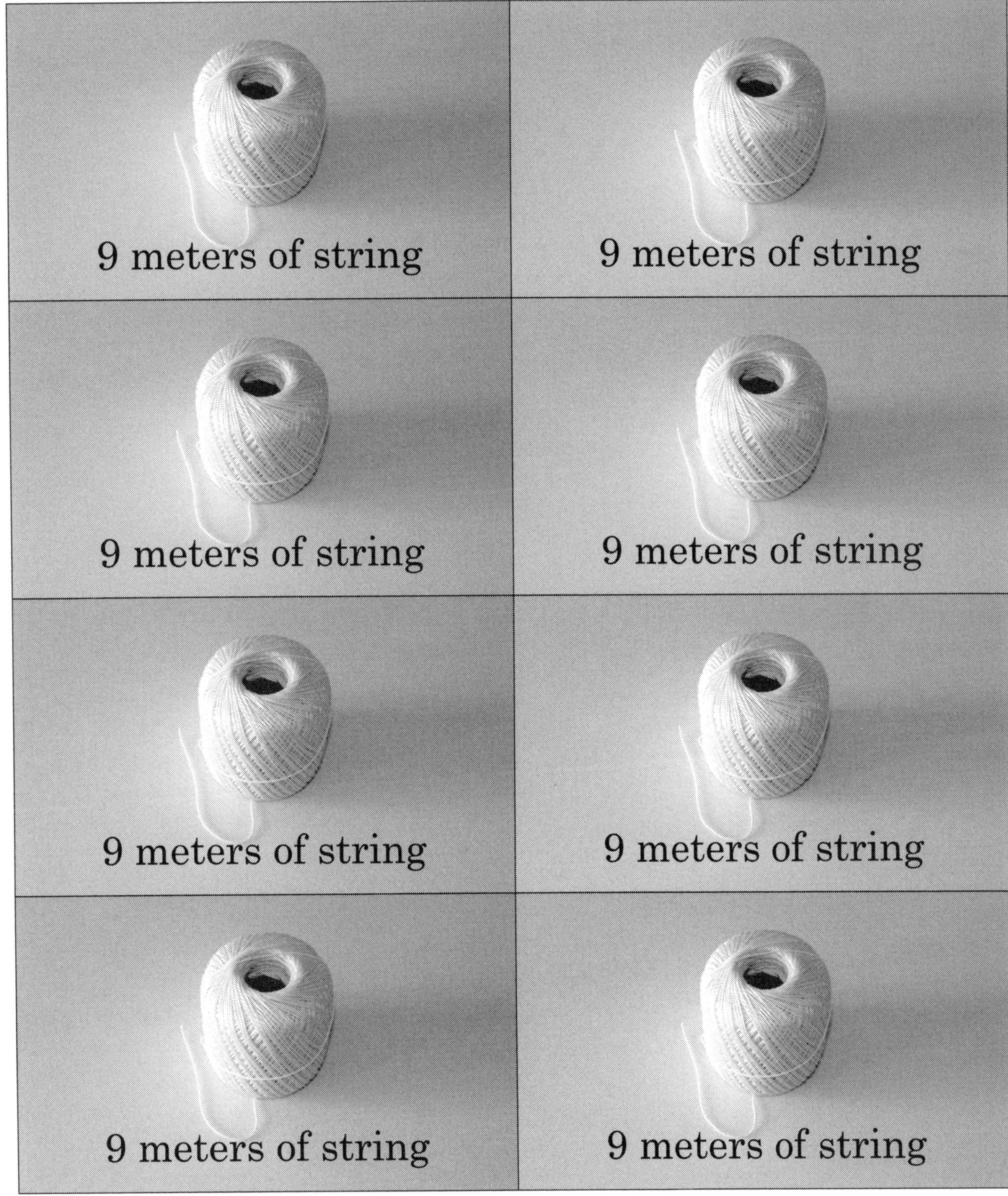

ACTIVITY 7.5 (continued)
INTERMEDIATE GOODS TICKETS

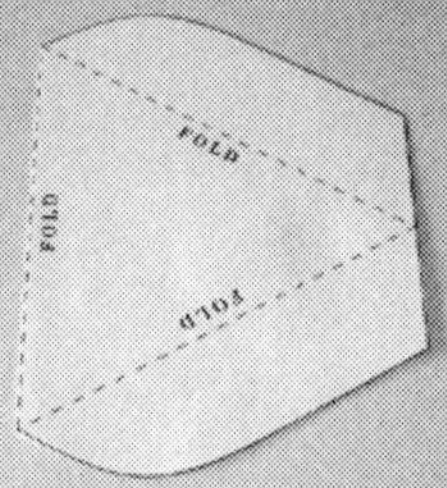

1 gore pattern	1 gore pattern
1 gore pattern	1 gore pattern
1 gore pattern	1 gore pattern
1 gore pattern	1 gore pattern

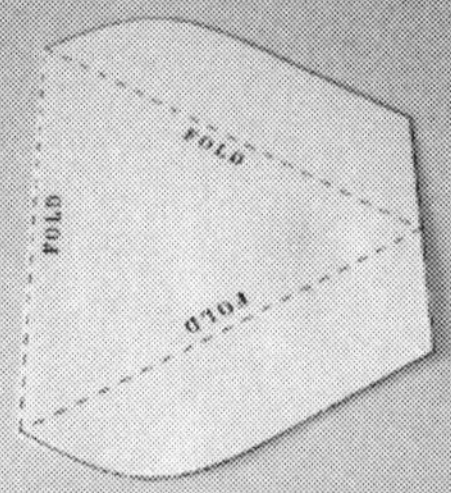

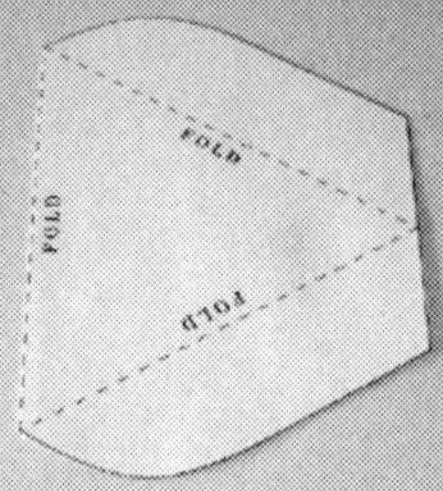

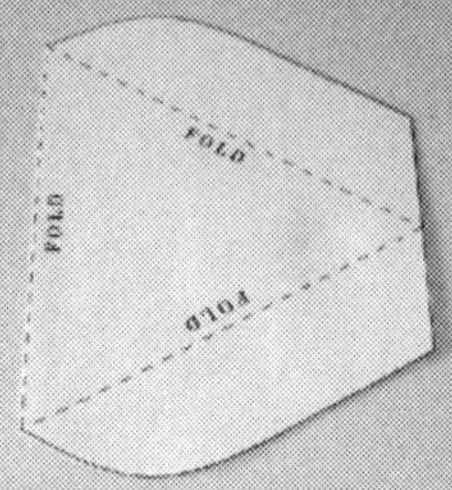

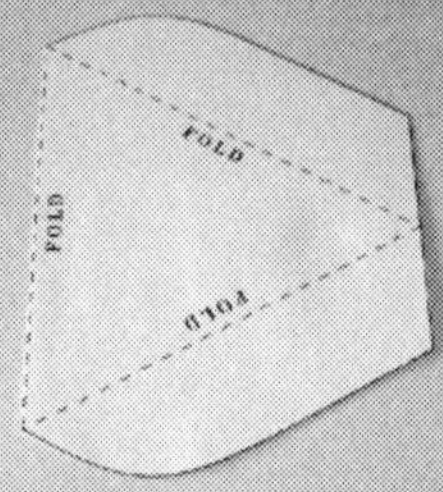

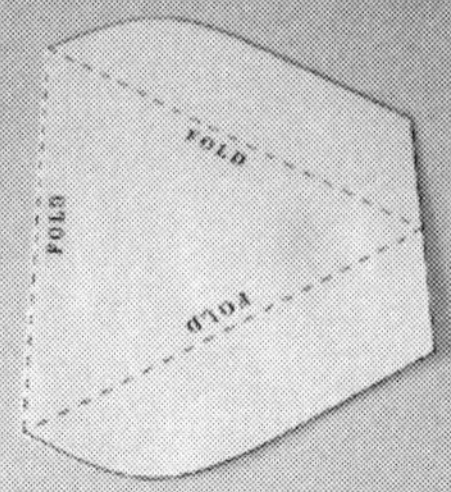

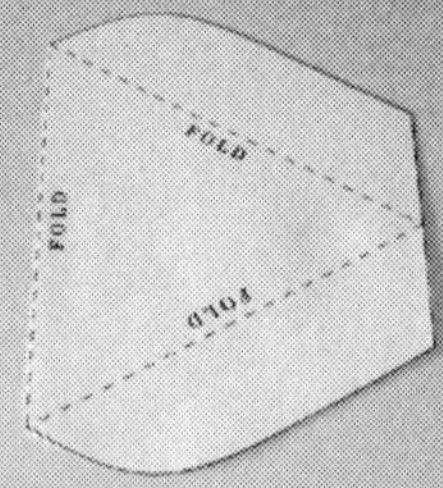

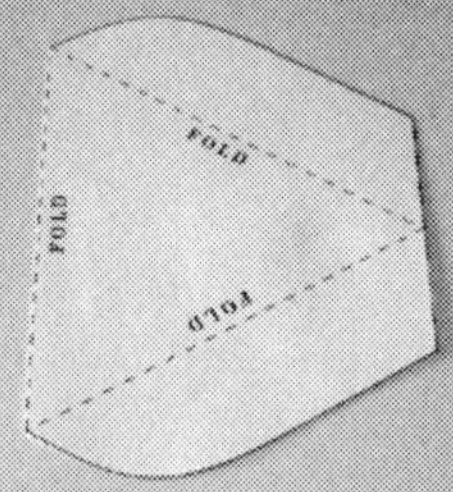

ACTIVITY 7.5 (continued)
INTERMEDIATE GOODS TICKETS

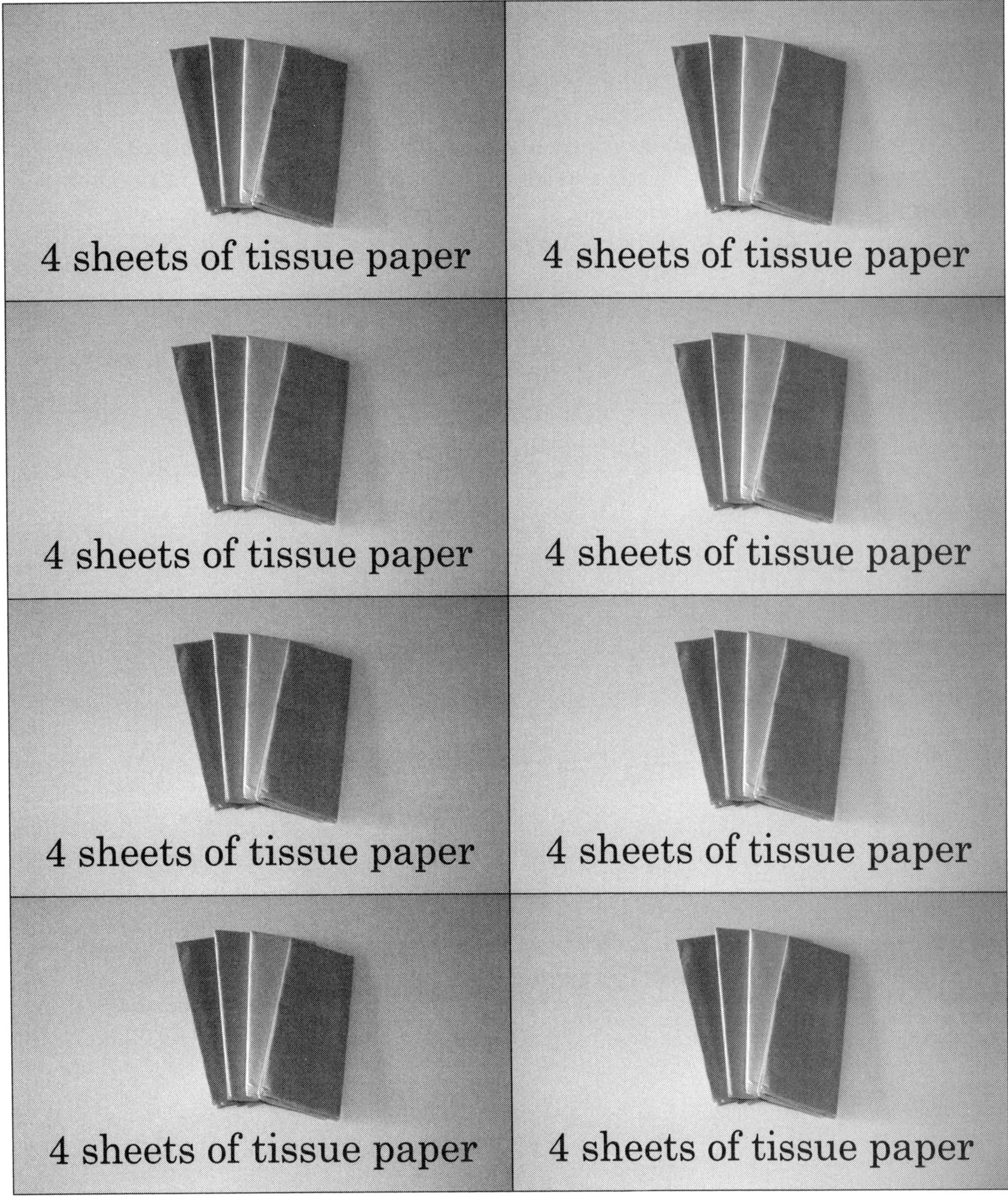

ACTIVITY 7.6
ASSESSMENT: SHAPELY LUNCH

Directions: Luis, Michael and Sonya hurry from math class into the cafeteria for lunch. As they empty their lunch sacks, Sonya notices that many of their items look like the shapes they have just been studying.

"Hey!" Sonya exclaims, "Look at our lunches. Everything we have looks like the shapes in math class." Luis and Michael notice, too, and start to giggle. "Wouldn't it be fun," says Michael, "if we all ate the same 'shapely' lunch?" They agree and decide to do some bartering.

Here is what each student brought for lunch:

Luis	**Michael**	**Sonya**
• Italian meatballs	• Yogurt	• PB&J sandwich
• Pretzels	• Orange	• Pickle
• Peach	• Small can of chips	• Brownie
• Can of root beer	• Carton of milk	• Juice box

1. Which three lunch items look like a cylinder?

2. Which three items look like a rectangular prism?

3. Which three items look like a sphere?

ACTIVITY 7.6 (continued)
ASSESSMENT: SHAPELY LUNCH

4. Fill in the blanks below to explain how Luis, Michael and Sonya can barter
    their lunch items so that they each have a cylinder, a rectangular prism
    and a sphere.

A. Luis has two lunch items that are the same shape:

________________________ and a ________________________.

He needs to barter for a ______________________ shape, so he barters

a ____________________ for a ______________________.

B. Michael has two lunch items that are the same shape:

a ______________________ and a ______________________.

He needs to barter for a ______________________ shape, so he barters

a ______________________ for a ______________________.

C. Sonya has three lunch items that are the same shape:

a ______________________, a ______________________

and a ________________. She needs to barter for two different shapes:

a ______________________ and a ______________________.

She first barters a ______________________ for

a ______________________ and then barters

a __________________ for a ______________________.

ACTIVITY 7.6 (continued)
ASSESSMENT: SHAPELY LUNCH

5. Draw a picture of what each student actually ate for lunch.

<table>
<tr><td>Luis

</td></tr>
<tr><td>Michael

</td></tr>
<tr><td>Sonya

</td></tr>
</table>

Lesson 8 - Doughnut Dreaming

OVERVIEW

This lesson focuses on demand (economics) and line graphs (mathematics). The students use a class survey to collect data about the quantity demanded of doughnuts at different prices. They use this data to construct a line graph. They discuss the law of demand and apply it to the graph to understand that at lower prices, the students will purchase more doughnuts.

CONCEPTS

Economics
> Demand
> Law of demand

Mathematics
> Decimals
> Line graphs
> Operations

CONTENT STANDARDS

Economics
Standard 8
The Voluntary National Content Standards in Economics place the benchmark for demand at the 8th grade level. Many district elementary economics curricula introduce this concept in the lower grades, so we have chosen to include it in this lesson.

> • **Benchmark 1 for 4th grade:** Higher prices for a good or service provide incentives for buyers to purchase less of that good or service and for producers to make or sell more of it. Lower prices for a good or service provide incentives for buyers to purchase more of that good or service and for producers to make or sell less of it.
> • **Benchmark 1 for 8th grade:** An increase in the price of a good or service encourages people to look for substitutes, causing the quantity demanded to decrease and vice versa. This relationship between price and quantity demanded, known as the law of demand, exists as long as other factors influencing demand do not change.

Mathematics
Data Analysis and Probability
> • Collect data using observations, surveys and experiments.
> • Represent data using tables and graphs such as line plots, bar graphs and line graphs.
> • Propose and justify conclusions and predictions that are based on data, and design studies to further investigate the conclusions or predictions.

Connections
> • Recognize and apply mathematics in contexts outside of mathematics.

OBJECTIVES

The students will:
1. Collect data using a survey.

2. Create a line graph using information from a survey.

3. Interpret information from a line graph illustrating demand for a product.

4. Explain the role of prices in the law of demand.

TIME REQUIRED

60 minutes

MATERIALS

1. Visuals 8.1, 8.2, 8.3 and 8.4
   (**Note**: Visual 8.1 and Activity 8.1 are the same and Visual 8.4 and Activity 8.2 are the same)

2. One copy of Activities 8.1, 8.2 and 8.3 for each student

3. Rulers

4. **Optional:** Doughnuts and a newspaper

ADDITIONAL RESOURCES

For additional curriculum connections, Web links, technology applications and suggested children's literature that will help you teach this lesson, go to
http://mathandecon.ncee.net/35/lesson8

PROCEDURE

1. Walk into the classroom holding a newspaper and eating a doughnut. Ask the students if they enjoy eating doughnuts. Discuss their favorite flavors of doughnuts and record on the board where they usually purchase them. Ask if they know how often they buy doughnuts, and discuss other ideas about doughnuts to interest them in the topic.

2. Tell the students to pretend that the newspaper says a new doughnut shop is opening up right down the street from the school. The shop will be called Daydream

Doughnuts. Ask the students to daydream for a moment about the smell, the sight and the taste of a warm doughnut coming out of the oven and to think about how much they love to eat doughnuts.

3. Now ask the students to daydream about the price of the doughnuts. Tell them the owners of the new shop don't know what to charge. Ask them if they are willing to help the owners.

4. Distribute a copy of Activity 8.1 to each student and display Visual 8.1. Tell the students to pretend that they receive a $10 allowance each week. They must use this allowance to pay for all of their weekly expenses such as soft drinks, candy, ice cream, books, toys, movies and video games. Given this requirement, ask the students to decide how many doughnuts they would be willing and able to buy at each price during one week, using one week's allowance. Tell the students to think about plain doughnuts, not a fancy variety, so they realize that $1.50 might be considered a high price. Discuss this example with the class:

    If I spent my entire $10 allowance on doughnuts, how many would I be able to buy during one week at the price of $1.50 each? I would be able to buy six doughnuts, but am I willing to spend all my allowance on doughnuts?

5. Have the students work through the calculations for all the prices and record in the second column of the table the number of doughnuts they would be able to buy with their $10. Go over the answers with the students and fill in the second column on the visual. ***At $1.50, they would be able to buy six doughnuts; at $1.25, eight doughnuts; at $1.00, 10 doughnuts; at $0.75, 13 doughnuts; at $0.50, 20 doughnuts and at $0.25, 40 doughnuts.***

6. Remind the students that they may have other wants and would be willing to buy only one doughnut at $1.50. Ask them to

raise their hands and volunteer the number of doughnuts they might be willing to buy at this price. Tell them to write this number in the appropriate space in the third column of the table and to fill in the rest of the third column with the number of doughnuts they would be willing to buy with their $10 at each of the other prices. Remind them that each person's answer may be different. Tell them to make their calculations on the bottom of the page. (**Note:** Make sure the students understand that if they would be willing and able to buy three doughnuts at $1.00 each, they also would be willing and able to buy at least three doughnuts at the lower prices of $0.75, $0.50 and $0.25. If a buyer is willing to buy a doughnut at a certain price level, logically the buyer will also buy at least as many doughnuts at all the lower prices.)

7.   Using Visual 8.2, compile the data from each student's survey to obtain a class

total of the number of doughnuts demanded at each price. To speed up the process, number each student, call out each number and ask the student how many doughnuts he or she would be willing and able to buy at each price. Assign a student volunteer to add the class quantities for one price and enter the total on the demand schedule to assist in recording the class totals at each price. See the table for an example of a completed class demand schedule.

8.   Ask the students to look at the findings from the class survey on Visual 8.2. What can they conclude? *People wanted fewer doughnuts when the price was high. At $0.25 for each doughnut, the students wanted more doughnuts than they wanted at $1.50 each.*

9.   Display Visual 8.3. Explain that in economics, the term **demand** refers to the schedule of the quantity of a good or service, in this case doughnuts, that people are willing and able to buy at different prices during a given time period. According to the **law of demand**, people are willing and able to buy less of a good or service at a higher price and more of a good or service at a lower price, when income and prices of other items remain the same.
(**Note**: **Demand** is the whole schedule or relationship, while the number purchased at each price is the **quantity demanded** at that price.)

10. Ask the following questions:
    A. What are the different prices for doughnuts? *$1.50, $1.25, $1.00, $0.75, $0.50 and $0.25*
    B. What was the time period of the survey? *One week*
    C. Share examples of other products you have observed that follow the law of demand: People buy more when the prices are lower. *Answers will vary and include CDs, video games, candy bars and grocery items. For example, when*

Class Demand Schedule						
Price	$0.25	$0.50	$0.75	$1.00	$1.25	$1.50
Student 1	40	20	5	3	1	0
Student 2	30	10	8	7	5	4
Student 3	30	5	6	5	4	2
Student 4	40	7	6	5	3	1
Student 5	25	8	5	3	0	0
Student 6	21	10	10	8	6	6
Student 7	20	20	7	6	5	2
Student 8	20	8	9	7	5	3
Student 9	10	10	7	5	5	4
Student 10	5	4	9	8	6	5
Student 11	10	9	9	7	5	5
Student 12	10	10	5	3	1	0
Student 13	15	15	5	3	2	1
Student 14	20	12	7	5	4	2
Student 15	25	17	7	6	4	3
Student 16	22	18	8	7	6	5
Student 17	26	13	7	6	5	4
Student 18	30	19	8	6	5	5
Student 19	26	11	10	9	7	5
Total	425	226	138	109	79	57

oranges or apples go on sale at the grocery store, people buy more of them because the price is lower.

11. Tell the students they will now plot the data from the class demand schedule on a line graph. Distribute a copy of Activity 8.2 to each student and display Visual 8.4. Use the visual to demonstrate each step as the students work through the graph. Identify and review the basic elements of a graph: title, horizontal (or X) axis, vertical (or Y) axis, points and line.

12. Tell the students to label the horizontal axis "Quantity of Doughnuts," and label each interval on this axis in number increments appropriate to the results of the class survey. Help them with this by determining the increments based on the total demanded at $0.25. Then tell them to label the vertical axis "Price per Doughnut," and label the intervals on this axis with the doughnut prices from $1.50 at the top to $0.
(**Note:** It may seem unusual to have price on the vertical axis and quantity demanded on the horizontal axis, but in economics, it is standard procedure. This is different from the typical graphing of a functional relationship in mathematics: The horizontal axis (X) is usually the domain, the vertical axis (Y) is usually the range and Y is a function of X.)

13. Ask the class to create a new title for the graph. *Answers will vary; make sure the students include the idea of demand for doughnuts in their titles.*

14. Using Visual 8.4, guide the students through plotting each point in the class demand schedule on the graph. Use the following example to get them started:
    Assume that class demand for doughnuts at $1.50 each is 20 doughnuts. Find the place on the graph where $1.50 and 20 intersect and make a point.
Show the students how to plot the first data point and then let them work with

partners or independently to plot the rest of the points. Once the students have finished, give each one a ruler and tell them to connect the points to create a demand line. Have them label the line **D** for demand, and tell them that economists refer to this line as a **demand curve**.

15. Ask the students what they have created. *A line graph* Tell them they have also created what economists call a **demand graph** that illustrates the law of demand. Remind the students that according to the law of demand, people are willing and able to buy less of a good or service at a higher price and more of a good or service at a lower price, when income and prices of other items remain the same. Review the activity with the class as they look at their graphs by asking the following questions:
    A. What things were the same in the data we collected? *$10 allowance, one-week time period*
    B. Do your graphs illustrate the law of demand? *Yes*
    C. Who would like to explain this answer? *Answers will vary but the student should know that at higher prices, the class demanded a smaller number of doughnuts; and at lower prices, they demanded more doughnuts. This shows that people were willing and able to buy more doughnuts at the lower prices.*
    D. Predict the quantity of doughnuts the class would demand at a price of $10.00 per doughnut. *Buyers would buy very few doughnuts at this price.*
    E. Predict the quantity of doughnuts the class would demand at $0.15 apiece. More or fewer than your graphs show? *More* How about $0.05 per doughnut? *Even more people would be willing and able to buy more doughnuts at this price.*

CLOSURE

16. Remind the students that today they have analyzed doughnut prices to advise the owners of the new doughnut shop. They have learned how to take survey information and create a demand graph to make a picture of the survey data. Ask the following questions:

A. What is **demand**? *The schedule of the quantity of a good or service that people are willing and able to buy at different prices during a given time period*

B. Look at your graphs and explain what you learned about the relationship between price and quantity of doughnuts demanded. *As the price of an item goes down, the quantity, or number, of items demanded increases. As the price rises, the quantity demanded decreases.*

C. Identify the important elements of a line graph. *Title, horizontal (or X) axis, vertical (or Y) axis, points and lines*

D. Who can list the steps necessary to create a line graph? *Gather data and check for accuracy, create a title, label the X-axis and the Y-axis, plot the data points and use a ruler to connect the points.*

E. What advice is the class going to give the owners of the doughnut shop? *Answers will vary but should include the inverse relationship between price and quantity demanded.*

ASSESSMENT

Distribute a copy of Activity 8.3 to each student. Review the instructions, give the students time to work, and go over the answers when they have finished.
(**Note:** The students can do this activity as a homework assignment, as practice in pairs or as a general review of line graphs.)

A. How many pencils did people want to buy at $0.70? *30* How many more pencils did people want to buy at $0.50 than at $0.70? *20 more*

B. How many pencils do you think people would want to buy if the pencils were $1.50 each? *0* How many pencils do you think people would want to buy if the pencils were $0.05 each? *Answers will vary but should be more than 100.*

C. Define demand. *The schedule of the number of items people are willing and able to buy at different prices during a given time period*

D. How does the graph illustrate the law of demand? *At lower prices, people will be willing and able to buy more items; at higher prices, people will be willing and able to buy fewer items.*

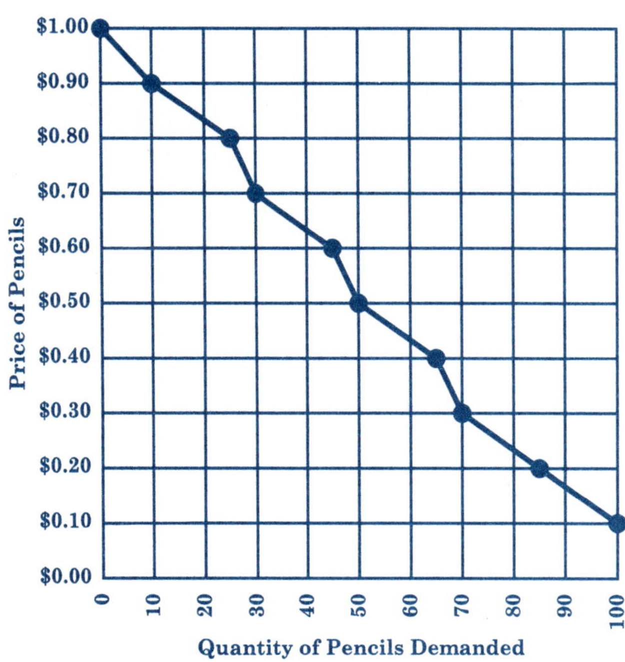

E. What advice will you give the inventor about the price for a Power Pencil? *Answers will vary but should include the inverse relationship between price and quantity demanded.*

VISUAL 8.1
MY DEMAND SCHEDULE FOR DAYDREAM DOUGHNUTS

Directions: Pretend you receive a weekly $10 allowance. Although you might want to spend all $10 on doughnuts, remember that your $10 allowance must pay for all of your expenses during the week, such as soft drinks, ice cream, books, toys, movies, video games and donations. Record the number of doughnuts you would be willing and able to buy at each price during one week, using one week's allowance. Remember, if you are willing and able to buy a number of doughnuts at a certain price, you should be willing and able to buy at least this same number of doughnuts — and probably more — at any lower price.

Price per Doughnut	Able to Buy	Willing to Buy
$1.50		
$1.25		
$1.00		
$0.75		
$0.50		
$0.25		

VISUAL 8.2
OUR CLASS DEMAND SCHEDULE FOR DAYDREAM DOUGHNUTS

Price	$0.25	$0.50	$0.75	$1.00	$1.25	$1.50
Student 1						
Student 2						
Student 3						
Student 4						
Student 5						
Student 6						
Student 7						
Student 8						
Student 9						
Student 10						
Student 11						
Student 12						
Student 13						
Student 14						
Student 15						
Student 16						
Student 17						
Student 18						
Student 19						
Total						

VISUAL 8.3
DEMAND AND THE LAW OF DEMAND

Demand: The schedule of the quantity of a good or service that people are willing and able to buy at different prices during a given time period

Law of demand: People are willing and able to buy less of a good or service at a higher price and more of a good or service at a lower price, when income and prices of other items remain the same.

VISUAL 8.4
A LINE GRAPH

Title: ____

ACTIVITY 8.1
MY DEMAND SCHEDULE FOR DAYDREAM DOUGHNUTS

Directions: Pretend you receive a weekly $10 allowance. Although you might want to spend all $10 on doughnuts, remember that your $10 allowance must pay for all of your expenses during the week, such as soft drinks, ice cream, books, toys, movies, video games and donations. Record the number of doughnuts you would be willing and able to buy at each price during one week, using one week's allowance. Remember, if you are willing and able to buy a number of doughnuts at a certain price, you should be willing and able to buy at least this same number of doughnuts — and probably more — at any lower price.

Price per Doughnut	Able to Buy	Willing to Buy
$1.50		
$1.25		
$1.00		
$0.75		
$0.50		
$0.25		

ACTIVITY 8.2
A LINE GRAPH

Title: ____

ACTIVITY 8.3
ASSESSMENT: POWER PENCILS

Directions: An inventor has created a Power Pencil and wants your help to fig-ure out how much to charge for it. Use the demand schedule on the next page to create a line graph for the inventor, showing the demand for the new pencils.

1. Label the horizontal axis of the graph on the next page "Quantity of Pencils Demanded." Label the lines on the horizontal axis by tens from 0 to 100.

2. Label the vertical axis "Price of Pencils." Label the lines on the vertical axis by units of $0.10 from $0 to $1.00.

3. Plot the data points from the demand schedule on the next page on the graph and connect the points with a line.

4. Label the graph "A Demand Graph for Power Pencils."

5. Answer the following questions:
     A. How many Power Pencils did people want to buy at $0.70? _________
     How many more did people want to buy at $0.50 than at $0.70? _________

     B. How many Power Pencils do you think people would want to buy if the pencils were $1.50 each? _________
     How many do you think people would want to buy if the pencils were $0.05 each? _________

     C. Define demand.

     D. How does the graph illustrate the law of demand?

     E. What advice will you give the inventor about the price for a Power Pencil?

ACTIVITY 8.3 (continued)
ASSESSMENT: POWER PENCILS

Demand Schedule	
Price per Pencil	Quantity Demanded
$1.00	0
$0.90	10
$0.80	25
$0.70	30
$0.60	45
$0.50	50
$0.40	65
$0.30	70
$0.20	85
$0.10	100

Title:____

Lesson 9 - How Much Time?

OVERVIEW

This lesson focuses on opportunity cost (economics) and graphs (mathematics). The students review terms related to measuring time and convert a time schedule into a pie chart, or circle graph. The students use the circle graph to assist them in making decisions about using time wisely to satisfy the requirements of a school-day schedule, and they consider the opportunity cost of their decisions.

CONCEPTS

Economics
> Alternatives
> Choice
> Goods
> Opportunity cost
> Services

Mathematics
> Creating and interpreting a circle graph
> Reading a table
> Time segments

CONTENT STANDARDS

Economics
Standard 1
- **Benchmark 1 for 4th grade:** People make choices because they cannot have everything they want.
- **Benchmark 5 for 4th grade:** People's choices about what goods and services to buy and consume determine how resources will be used.
- **Benchmark 6 for 4th grade:** Whenever a choice is made, something is given up.
- **Benchmark 7 for 4th grade:** The opportunity cost of a choice is the value of the best alternative given up.

Mathematics
Measurement
- Understand measurable attributes of objects and the units, systems and processes of measurement (time).
Representation
- Create and use representations to organize, record and communicate mathematical ideas (tables and graphs).
Connections
- Recognize and apply mathematics in contexts outside of mathematics.

OBJECTIVES

The students will:
1. Read information on a table.

2. Create a circle graph using information from a table.

3. Make simple conversions between minutes, hours and days.

4. Give an example of an opportunity cost after they make a choice.

TIME REQUIRED

60 minutes

MATERIALS

1. Visuals 9.1 and 9.2

2. One copy of Activities 9.1 and 9.2 for each student

3. Transparency pens in the following colors: orange, yellow, brown, pink, green, red, blue, purple, black

4. Coloring tools for each student in the following colors: orange, yellow, brown, pink, green, red, blue, purple, black (There must be at least two choices available for all the students, such as markers, crayons or colored pencils.)

ADDITIONAL RESOURCES

For additional curriculum connections, Web links, technology applications and suggested children's literature that will help you teach this lesson, go to http://mathandecon.ncee.net/35/lesson9

PROCEDURE

1. Ask the class to define **time**. *Answers will vary and include when things happen, a system of measuring, a period of existence in the world, any specified or defined period, what a clock shows, the duration of an event or action and how long something takes.*

2. Display Visual 9.1 and ask the following questions:
   A. What do you see? *Two clocks; one is an analog clock and one is a digital clock. The students may not know that the round clock is called an analog clock, but they will know it is a clock.*
   B. What time do the clocks show? *They both show 3:30.*
   C. Is it 3:30 a.m. or 3:30 p.m.? *Most students will say they cannot tell by looking only at the clock.*

   D. What do a.m. and p.m. mean? *A.M. means morning, the time between midnight and noon. A.M is short for the Latin term ante meridian. P.M. means past morning, the time between noon and midnight. P.M. is short for the Latin term post meridian.*

3. Ask the students the following questions:
   A. How many hours are in a day? *24 hours*
   B. How many minutes are in an hour? *60 minutes*
   C. How many minutes are in one half of an hour? *30 minutes*
   D. How many minutes are in one quarter of an hour? *15 minutes*
   E. How many minutes are in three quarters of an hour? *45 minutes*
   F. If there are 60 minutes in an hour and 24 hours in a day, how could you find out the number of minutes in a day? *Multiply 24 times 60*
   G. Work the problem and tell me how many minutes are in a day. *1,440*
   H. If a school day starts at 8:00 a.m. and ends at 3:00 p.m., how many hours are in the school day? *Seven hours*
   I. If there are seven hours in a school day, how many minutes are in the school day? *7 x 60 = 420 minutes*

4. Tell the students that even if people use the same clocks to measure time, no two people use their time exactly the same way. Tell them they are going to use school time as an example. All teachers are required to teach each day, but they have some discretion in how they allocate the seven hours (420 minutes) of a school day. Most teachers do not use their class time in exactly the same way. Tell the students to pretend the school has a beginning teacher named Mr. Sanchez. He has asked the class to help him make some decisions about his schedule. Show Visual 9.2. Tell the students that this is Mr. Sanchez's schedule for Tuesday of each week. The periods of time cannot be changed; they are required by the school.

(**Note:** You may wish to use your own or another teacher's name instead of "Mr. Sanchez.")

5. Tell the students to look at the table. It shows that Mr. Sanchez has opening exercises for 30 minutes, from 8:00 a.m. to 8:30 a.m. Next he has reading class from 8:30 a.m. to 9:30 a.m. How many minutes is reading class? *60 minutes* Write 60 in the "Minutes" column. Ask the students the number of minutes in each of the rest of the schedule sections and record their answers. Discuss the schedule with the students by asking these questions:

   A. Are there similarities between your school day and Mr. Sanchez's schedule? *Answers will vary but there should be some similarities, such as the same subjects each day, lunch and extracurricular activities.*

   B. How does your day differ from Mr. Sanchez's? *Answers will vary depending on the students' class schedule and their grade level.*

   C. At what time does Mr. Sanchez's open period begin? *1:00 p.m.*

   D. What subject does he teach just before the open period? *Social studies*

   E. What time does the next class begin after the open period? *2:00 p.m.*

   F. What is the class after the open period? *Science*

   G. How long is Mr. Sanchez's open period? *60 minutes*

   H. What is another way to express 60 minutes when we refer to time? *One hour*

6. Tell the students that Mr. Sanchez wants help deciding how to schedule his open period. Give each student a copy of Activity 9.1, and let them choose a coloring tool. Tell the students they are going to transfer the information from the table on Visual 9.2 to the circle graph on Activity 9.1 to help them more easily assist Mr. Sanchez. Explain to the students that the circle represents seven hours, and it has been divided into 30-minute, or half-hour, sections. Ask the fol-

lowing questions:

   A. Count the number of sections on the circle graph. How many are there? *14*

   B. If there are 14 sections and each represents 30 minutes, how would you find out how many minutes all the sections represent? *Multiply the number of sections times the amount of time each section represents: 14 x 30.*

   C. How many minutes does the entire graph represent? *420 minutes*

7. Remind the students that it takes two 30-minute sections, or two half hours, to equal 60 minutes or one full hour.

   • Make the "Color" box in the first row of the table on Visual 9.2 orange, and tell the students to use orange to color the number of sections needed to represent the opening exercises. Show the students how to fill in one section to represent the first 30-minute period. Have the students check each other to make sure they are doing the activity correctly.

   • Make the "Reading" color box yellow, and tell the students to use yellow to color the number of sections needed to represent the time spent in reading. Tell them not to skip a section between the opening exercises and reading. When they have finished, ask them how many sections they colored to represent the time allocated to reading. *Two sections = 60 minutes*

   • Make the "Language Arts" color box brown, and tell the students to use brown to color the sections representing language arts. When they have finished, ask them how many sections they colored brown. *One section = 30 minutes*

8. After checking to make sure the students are following the instructions correctly, mark the remaining color boxes as indicated below, and have the students complete the circle graph. Remind them not to skip sections of the graph.
   • Breaks: pink
   • Math: green
   • Writing: red
   • Lunch: pink

- Social Studies: blue
- Open period: no color
- Science: purple
- Prepare to depart: black

9. Ask the following questions:
   A. How many sections did they color pink? *Two*
   B. How much time does Mr. Sanchez's class spend eating lunch and taking breaks? *One hour*
   C. How many sections did they leave blank to represent the time Mr. Sanchez wants help deciding how to use? *Two*
   D. How much time do these two sections represent? *60 minutes or an hour*

10. Tell the students that Mr. Sanchez's choices for how to use these 60 minutes are listed under the circle graph:
    - 60-minute gym class
    - 30 minutes in the computer lab
    - 30-minute music lesson
    - 30-minute art lesson
    - 30-minute library book check-out period
    - 30-minute pleasure reading of the students' choice

    Write the word **alternatives** on the board. Explain to the students that this is another word for all the possible choices a person has when making a decision. Review Mr. Sanchez's six alternatives by listing them under the word "alternatives" on the board in the same order they are listed on Activity 9.1, with the time next to each. (You could also list the alternatives and times on a transparency under the word "alternatives.")

11. Ask the following questions:
    A. Can Mr. Sanchez schedule all his alternatives during the open period? Why? *No, because there is not enough time to do everything*
    B. If he chooses the gym class, can he schedule any of the other activities? *No, because the class requires 60 minutes, and this is all the time he has open*
    C. Can he schedule all of the 30-minute activities? *No*
    D. How much time would he need for any three of the 30-minute activities? *He would need 90 minutes.*
    E. Can he schedule two of the 30-minute activities? Why? *Yes, because two 30-minute activities take 60 minutes, and he has an hour available.*

12. Tell the students to look at the alternatives and choose how they would suggest Mr. Sanchez allocate the time. Tell them to circle their choice, or choices, on the bottom of Activity 9.1. Have the students use partners to check each other to see that everyone has circled activities that will fit in the time available.

13. Call out each alternative and ask the students to raise their hand when you get to their choice, or choices, for Mr. Sanchez's open period. Count the hands and record the numbers beside each alternative on the blackboard or visual. For each alternative, ask a few students to share the reason why they made this choice. Remind the students that if they picked the 60-minute gym class, this should have been their only choice. The students who chose one of the 30-minute activities should have also picked another 30-minute activity to completely fill the open period.

14. Tell the students to look at all the alternatives and the votes. Ask them if there is a clear winner. *This will depend on how the students voted.* Remind the students that people picked different alternatives because we do not all use our time the same way. We are different and use our time differently to satisfy our wants.

15. Ask the students to look at the list of alternatives again. If they had more time and could choose just one more activity, which one would they choose? Tell the students to write this alternative on the bottom of their paper.

16. Write the words **opportunity cost** on the board. Explain to the students that the activity they wrote on the bottom of their paper is the opportunity cost of the choice they made when they made a final selection for Mr. Sanchez's schedule during his open period. Tell the students that opportunity cost is the next best alternative they gave up. Ask some of the students to share their opportunity cost. ***Answers will vary, because not all of us make the same choices, nor do we have the same opportunity costs.***
(**Note:** Because the gym class is 60 minutes, the opportunity cost of this choice will be the two next best 30-minute activities the students chose.)

17. Call out each of Mr. Sanchez's alternatives again, and ask the students to raise their hand when you get to the opportunity cost they wrote on the bottom of their paper. Count the hands and record the numbers beside each alternative on the blackboard or visual. Tell the students to notice that, just as all of them did not make the same choice for Mr. Sanchez, they also did not all have the same opportunity cost.

18. Ask the students what they used to color the circle graph. ***Answers will vary depending on the coloring tools that were available.*** Tell the students they had an opportunity cost when they chose which coloring tool to use: If they chose to use markers and their next choice would have been crayons, then crayons were the opportunity cost of their choice to use markers. Tell the students that they have an opportunity cost every time they make choices among alternative **goods** — objects that can satisfy wants — and alternative **services** — actions that can satisfy wants.

CLOSURE

19. Discuss the following review questions with the students:
   A. How many minutes are in an hour? ***60 minutes***
   B. How many minutes are in one half hour? ***30 minutes***
   C. How many minutes are in one quarter of an hour? ***15 minutes***
   D. Are two quarters of an hour the same as one half hour? Why? ***Yes, because one quarter plus one quarter is one half. One half hour is 30 minutes, and two quarters of an hour equal 30 minutes.***
   E. How many minutes are in three quarters of an hour? ***45 minutes***
   F. How many minutes are between 9:15 and 10:00? ***45 minutes***
   G. How many quarter hours are in one hour? ***Four***
   H. Sean has 30 minutes before dinner; and he wants to practice basketball shots, watch television and ride his bicycle each for 30 minutes. Can he do all three of these activities? Why? ***No, it would take one and a half hours to do all three.***
   I. What is another word for Sean's three choices? ***Alternatives***
   J. Sean decides to ride his bicycle; but if he could do one more thing, he would watch television. What is Sean's opportunity cost? ***Watching television***
   K. You have to decide between your two favorite snacks: an apple or peanuts. You choose peanuts. What is the apple? ***The apple is your opportunity cost.***

ASSESSMENT

Distribute Activity 9.2 to each student and allow them time to complete it in class or assign it as homework. Go over the answers with the students.

1. Number these activities from least to greatest amount of time needed, starting with 1 for the activity that takes the least amount of time.
   2 Skating: 30 minutes
   1 Playing a video game: One quarter of an hour
   3 Hiking: Three quarters of an hour
   4 Watching television: One hour

2. Tamara wants to go shopping for 45 minutes. Circle the option that allows her at least 45 minutes at the mall.
   A. 2:00 p.m. to 2:15 p.m.
   B. 2:20 p.m. to 2:40 p.m.
   C. 2:25 p.m. to 3:30 p.m.
   D. 2:30 p.m. to 3:00 p.m.

3. Use the table below to answer these questions.
   A. What time does Juanita eat dinner? ***6:00 p.m.***
   B. How long does Juanita practice the piano? ***30 minutes or one half hour***

4. Use the circle graph below to answer these questions.
   A. This circle graph represents two hours at Washington School. How much time does each section of the graph represent? ***2 hours x 60 minutes = 120 minutes. 120/8 sections = 15 minutes or one quarter of an hour***
   B. How much time do the students spend in reading class? ***3 x 15 = 45 minutes or three quarters of an hour***

5. Read the paragraph below and then answer these questions.
   A. How long does Zack practice each day? ***20 x 3 = 60 minutes or one hour***
   B. Zack cannot do all of his practice activities tomorrow because he must go to the dentist. He has only 40 minutes and must skip one activity. Zack must make a choice. What are his alternatives? Which would you recommend he skip? ***His alternatives are batting, catching or running. The students will have different answers about which activity they recommend he skip.***
   C. On Thursday Zack can practice for only 20 minutes. He has decided to practice batting, but he would really like to have time to practice catching, too. What is his opportunity cost? ***Practicing catching***
   D. On the back of this paper, write at least three sentences about a choice you have made recently. Be sure to include your alternatives, the choice you made and your opportunity cost. ***Answers will vary, but look for correct use of the terms alternatives and opportunity cost.***

VISUAL 9.1
WHAT ARE THESE?

VISUAL 9.2
MR. SANCHEZ'S CLASS SCHEDULE FOR TUESDAY

Time	Activity	Minutes	Color
8:00 a.m. to 8:30 a.m.	Opening exercises		
8:30 a.m. to 9:30 a.m.	Reading		
9:30 a.m. to 10:00 a.m.	Language Arts		
10:00 a.m. to 10:30 a.m.	Break (recess)		
10:30 a.m. to 11:30 a.m.	Math		
11:30 a.m. to 12:00 p.m.	Writing		
12:00 p.m. to 12:30 p.m.	Lunch		
12:30 p.m. to 1:00 p.m.	Social Studies		
1:00 p.m. to 2:00 p.m.	Open		
2:00 p.m. to 2:30 p.m.	Science		
2:30 p.m. to 3:00 p.m.	Prepare to depart		

ACTIVITY 9.1
MR. SANCHEZ'S CLASS SCHEDULE FOR TUESDAY

Directions: This circle represents a seven-hour school day divided into 30-minute sections. Help Mr. Sanchez chose how to schedule his 60-minute open period.

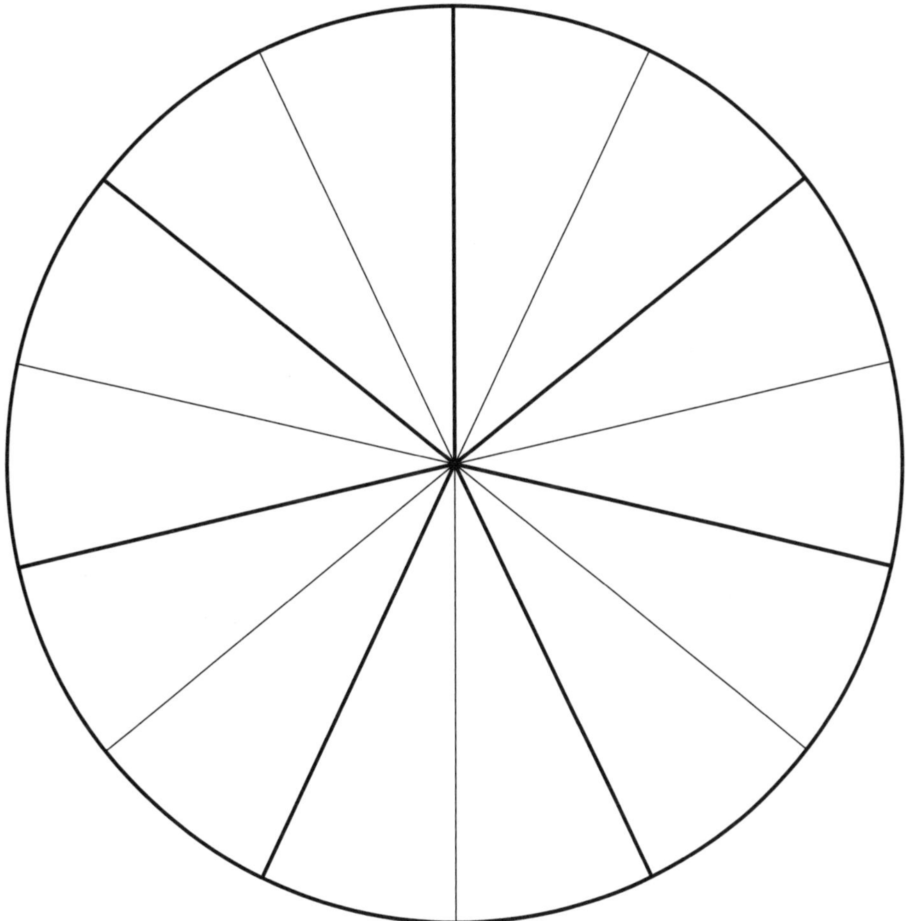

These are his choices:
- 60-minute gym class
- 30 minutes in the computer lab
- 30-minute music lesson
- 30-minute art lesson
- 30-minute library book check-out period
- 30-minute pleasure reading of the students' choice

Circle the choice(s) you would recommend for Mr. Sanchez's open period.

ACTIVITY 9.2
ASSESSMENT: WHAT DO YOU CHOOSE?

1. Number these activities from least to greatest amount of time needed, starting with 1 for the activity that takes the least amount of time.
   ____ Skating: 30 minutes
   ____ Playing a video game: One quarter of an hour
   ____ Hiking: Three quarters of an hour
   ____ Watching television: One hour

2. Tamara wants to go shopping for 45 minutes. Circle the option that allows her at least 45 minutes at the mall.
   A. 2:00 p.m. to 2:15 p.m.
   B. 2:20 p.m. to 2:40 p.m.
   C. 2:25 p.m. to 3:30 p.m.
   D. 2:30 p.m. to 3:00 p.m.

3. Use the table to answer the questions.
   A. What time does Juanita eat dinner?

   B. How long does Juanita practice the piano?

Juanita's After-School Schedule	
Time	**Activity**
4:00 p.m. to 4:15 p.m.	Eat a snack and change clothes
4:15 p.m. to 5:00 p.m.	Do homework
5:00 p.m. to 5:30 p.m.	Practice the piano
5:30 p.m. to 6:00 p.m.	Recreation
6:00 p.m. to 6:45 p.m.	Eat dinner

ACTIVITY 9.2 (continued)
ASSESSMENT: WHAT DO YOU CHOOSE?

4. Use the circle graph to answer the questions.

  A. This graph represents two hours at Washington School. How much time does each section of the graph represent?

  B. How much time do the students spend in reading class?

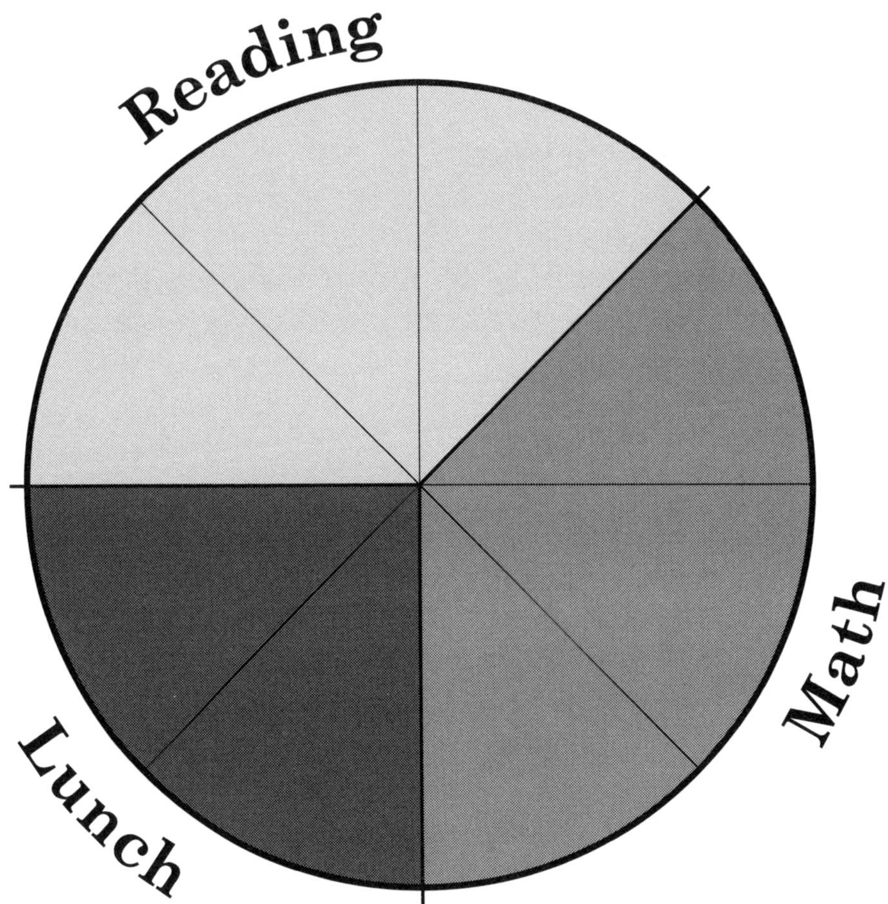

ACTIVITY 9.2 (continued)
ASSESSMENT: WHAT DO YOU CHOOSE?

5. Read the paragraph below and answer the questions.

Zack likes to play baseball. He wants to be a good player. He tries to practice every day after school. He practices batting for 20 minutes, catches the ball for 20 minutes and runs the bases for 20 minutes. Zack works very hard at trying to be a good baseball player.

A. How long does Zack practice each day?

B. Zack cannot do all of his practice activities tomorrow because he must go to the dentist. He has only 40 minutes and must skip one activity. Zack must make a choice. What are his alternatives? Which would you recommend he skip?

C. On Thursday Zack can practice for only 20 minutes. He has decided to practice batting, but he would really like to have time to practice catching, too. What is his opportunity cost?

D. On the back of this paper, write at least three sentences about a choice you have made recently. Be sure to include your alternatives, the choice you made and your opportunity cost.

Lesson 10 - Bunches of Brownies

OVERVIEW

This lesson focuses on resources (economics) and fractions (mathematics). The students use measuring cups to determine equivalent fractions for a recipe. Thinking economically, the students identify the productive resources they would use to make brownies and categorize them as natural resources, human resources or capital goods (resources). The students work in groups to decide how they would divide a pan of brownies equally. Finally, the students determine how much of each ingredient they would need if they wanted to produce additional batches of brownies.

CONCEPTS

Economics

    Capital goods (resources)
    Human resources
    Intermediate goods
    Natural resources
    Productive resources

Mathematics

    Fractions

CONTENT STANDARDS

Economics

Standard 1

- **Benchmark 9 for 4th Grade:** Productive resources are the natural resources, human resources and capital goods available to make goods and services.
- **Benchmark 10 for 4th grade:** Natural resources, such as land, are "gifts of nature"; they are present without human intervention.
- **Benchmark 11 for 4th grade:** Human resources are the quantity and quality of human effort directed toward producing goods and services.
- **Benchmark 12 for 4th grade:** Capital goods are goods produced and used to make other goods and services.

Mathematics

Number and operations

- Develop understanding of fractions as parts of unit wholes, as parts of a collection, as locations on number lines and as divisions of whole numbers.
- Develop and use strategies to estimate computations involving fractions and decimals in situations relevant to students' experience.

Problem Solving

- Solve problems that arise in mathematics and in other contexts.
- Apply and adapt a variety of appropriate strategies to solve problems.

Connections

- Recognize and apply mathematics in contexts outside of mathematics

OBJECTIVES

The students will:

1. Define productive resources and give examples of natural resources, human resources and capital goods (resources).

2. Define and give examples of intermediate goods.

3. Correctly use the terms fraction, denominator and numerator in context.

4. Identify equivalent fractions.

TIME REQUIRED

120 minutes

MATERIALS

1. Visuals 10.1 and 10.2

2. One copy of Activities 10.1, 10.2 and 10.3 for each student

3. One 2-inch x 6-inch strip of construction paper or a candy-bar wrapper with a solid line dividing it in half

4. One 2-inch x 6-inch strip of construction paper or a candy-bar wrapper with two solid lines dividing it in thirds

5. One 9-inch x 12-inch sheet of brown construction paper and a ruler for each group

6. Two pairs of scissors

7. A set of measuring cups that includes one-eighth, one-fourth, one-third, one-half, two-thirds, three-fourths and one cup; a pitcher or bowl; and a supply of rice, popcorn or small dry seeds for each group

ADDITIONAL RESOURCES

For additional curriculum connections, Web links, technology applications and suggested children's literature that will help you teach this lesson, go to http://mathandecon.ncee.net/35/lesson10

PROCEDURE

1. Tell the students that they are going to review **fractions** so they will be ready to do some cooking.

2. Explain that a fraction has a **numerator** and a **denominator**. Ask the students to suppose that they have a large chocolate-chip cookie divided into three equal parts. If they used a fraction to represent one part of this cookie, the denominator, or the number below the line in the fraction, would be 3 because the denominator represents the total number of equal parts in the whole. The numerator, or the number above the line in the fraction, would be 1, because the numerator in this example represents one equal part of the whole. Ask a volunteer to come to the board and write the fraction 1/3.

3. Divide the students into small groups. Remind the students that a fraction is part of a whole and that fractions allow people to divide a whole into equal parts. Each group in the class represents a fraction or part of the whole class. Discuss the following questions:
   A. If there are 24 students in the class, how many equal parts make up the whole class? *24*
   B. What is the denominator of a fraction that represents the students in the class? *24*
   C. If there are three students in a group, what is the numerator of the fraction that represents this group as one equal part of the whole class? *3*
   D. How would you write the fraction that represents the group of three students in the class of 24 students? *3/24 or 1/8*

4. Use examples based on the groups in the class for further review of denominator, numerator and fraction.

5. Write "1/3" and "1/2" on the board. Ask the students if you gave them part of a candy bar, would they rather have one-third or one-half of the candy bar? Why? *Answers will vary. Some of the students might recognize that one-half is larger than one-third.*

6. Show the students the two strips of construction paper (candy-bar wrappers), or pass the strips around the room so the students can see the lines on them. Explain that these two strips of paper represent candy bars. Ask two students to come to the front of the room. Give each student a pair of scissors and one of the paper candy bars. Have the students cut the paper candy bars along the solid lines. Ask one student to hold up one-half of the paper candy bar. Ask the other student to hold up one-third of the paper candy bar. Now ask which is larger and why. *One-half, because this fraction represents one part of two equal parts and one-third represents one part of three equal parts*

7. Pass a one-half strip and a one-third strip around the class so the students can compare the sizes.

8. Display Visual 10.1. Explain that this is a recipe for brownies. A recipe lists the ingredients required to prepare something such as cookies, casseroles and other food dishes. Discuss the following questions:
   A. Do you like brownies? Why? *Answers will vary.*
   B. Have you ever made brownies from a recipe such as this one? If not, how do you usually prepare brownies? *Buy and use a brownie mix to which someone adds a few ingredients such as eggs and water. Some students may say they buy brownies at a store.*

9. Distribute a copy of Activity 10.1 to each student and measuring cups, bowls or pitchers and rice to each group.

10. Review the instructions for the activity. Allow time for the students to work in their groups. When they have finished, discuss their answers.
   A. How many one-fourth-cup measures do you need for one full cup? How did you prove this? *Four. We filled the one-fourth-cup measure with rice*

and poured this rice into the one-cup measure. After four times, the one-cup measure was full.
   B. How many one-third-cup measures do you need to fill a two-thirds-cup measure? How did you prove this? *Two. We filled the one-third-cup measure and poured it into the two-thirds-cup measure. After two times, the two-thirds-cup measure was full.*
   C. How many one-eighth-cup measures must you use to make one-quarter cup? *Two* One-half cup? *Four* How did you prove this? *We filled the one-eighth-cup measure and poured it into the one-fourth-cup measure. We did this two times and the one-fourth-cup measure was full. We filled the one-eighth-cup measure and poured it into the one-half-cup measure. We did this four times and the one-half-cup measure was full.*
   D. Which is larger: one-eighth of a cup or one-fourth of a cup? How did you decide this? *One-fourth. It took two one-eighth-cup measures to fill one one-fourth-cup measure. So one-fourth of a cup is two times as large as one-eighth of a cup.*
   E. Write two sentences about fractions of a cup. *Answers will vary. Allow some students to share their sentences.*

11. Display Visual 10.1 again and explain that the recipe provides a list of the ingredients a person would need to produce brownies.

12. Explain that some of these ingredients are called **productive resources**. Define productive resources as the **natural resources**, **human resources** and **capital goods (resources)** that people use to produce a product. Discuss the following:
   • Natural resources such as land are "gifts of nature": They are present without human intervention.
   • Examples of natural resources include water and sunlight.
   • Ask the students for other examples of natural resources. *Answers will vary*

and could include trees, soil, coal, gold, crude oil and silver.
- Human resources are the quantity and quality of human effort directed toward producing goods and services.
- Examples of human resources include teachers, mechanics and bus drivers.
- Ask the students for other examples of human resources. *Answers will vary and could include doctors, baseball players, musicians, store clerks and custodians.*
- Capital goods are goods people produce and use to make other goods and services.
- Examples of capital goods include tools, tow trucks, school buses and business buildings.
- Ask the students for other examples of capital goods. *Answers will vary and could include power saws, hammers, cement trucks and the building for a grocery store.*

13. Refer the students to the ingredients on Visual 10.1. Ask them for other resources they would need to produce brownies. List their suggestions below the recipe. *Answers will vary and could include bowl, mixer, spoon, pan, oven, person to mix the ingredients, kitchen, electricity and water to wash the dishes.*

14. Have the students look at all the items listed on Visual 10.1 and ask them to find examples of natural resources, human resources and capital goods. *Natural resources: water and land the house or building is on. Human resource: person mixing the ingredients. Capital goods: oven, spoon, bowl, baking pan, mixer and other tools or pieces of equipment*

15. Explain that some of the items are things people use up when they produce brownies. These items are not natural resources because they do not occur naturally in or on the earth. They are not capital goods because people can't use them again and

again to produce something: They aren't tools and equipment. These items are **intermediate goods**: goods people use up in the production of something else.

16. Point out that flour is an intermediate good. People use it up in the production of the brownies: It stays in the brownies and can't be used again.

17. Distribute a copy of Activity 10.2 to each student. Tell the students to work with a partner and categorize each item on the activity as a natural resource, a human resource, a capital good or an intermediate good. Allow time for the students to work.

18. Display Visual 10.2 and ask the students to share their answers. Write their answers on the visual. *Natural resources: water, land the house or building is on. Human resources: person mixing ingredients. Capital goods: oven, spoon, bowl, mixer. Intermediate goods: flour, sugar, salt, chocolate powder, butter or oil, vanilla and egg*

19. Give each group a sheet of brown construction paper. Explain that it represents a whole pan of brownies. Tell the students to determine how they can divide the brownies equally among the members of their group by determining what fraction or part of the pan of brownies each member would receive.

20. Allow time for the students to work. Ask each group the following questions:
    A. How did you divide the pan of brownies? *Answers will vary. Encourage the students to use a fraction in their answers.*
    B. Why did you divide the pan of brownies in this way? *Answers will vary.*
    C. What part of the whole pan of brownies would each member of your group receive? *Answers will vary.*

21. Display Visual 10.1 again. Explain that the kindergarten teachers want to make

enough brownies to give each child one brownie. There are 36 students in kindergarten. If the teachers cut each pan of brownies into 12 pieces, how many pans of brownies will they need? *Three*

22. Ask the students how the kindergarten teachers will figure out how much of each ingredient they must buy to make three pans of brownies. *By adding each amount three times or multiplying it by three* Have the students work in their groups to do the calculations, and allow time for them to finish their work.

23. Ask a member from each group to share its answers. Write the correct amounts on the visual. *One and one-half cups of butter, three cups of sugar, three tablespoons of vanilla, six eggs, one and one-half cups of flour, one cup of cocoa, three-fourths of a teaspoon of baking powder and three-fourths of a teaspoon of salt*

CLOSURE

24. Ask the students:
    A. What is a fraction? *A part of a whole*
    B. If there are 24 students in the class and I divide them into three groups of eight, what fraction of the class does each group represent? *Eight twenty-fourths or one-third*

25. Ask the students to look at the class.
    A. How many people are in this class? *Answers will vary.*
    B. If we wanted half the class to stand, how many students would stand? *Half the number in the answer to the previous question*
    C. Ask this number of students to stand. Count the number of standing students and the number of sitting students to verify that each represents one-half of the class. Write the number of students equal to one-half the class and the fraction 1/2 on the board.

(**Note:** If you can't divide the class evenly for this question and Question 26, have the extra student(s) help by counting and writing the fractions on the board.)

26. Review with several more examples by having one-third, two-thirds and one-fourth of the class stand.

27. Continue reviewing the important content of the lesson by asking the following questions:
    A. What are natural resources? *Gifts of nature that are present without human intervention*
    B. Give examples of a natural resource. *Answers will vary and include water, trees and soil.*
    C. What are human resources? *The quantity and quality of human effort directed toward producing goods and services*
    D. Give examples of a human resource. *Answers will vary and include nurse, teacher, engineer, accountant and mechanic.*
    E. What are capital goods? *Answers will vary and include goods people produce and use to make other goods and services.*
    F. Give examples of capital goods. *Answers will vary and include tools, machines, equipment and factories.*
    G. What are intermediate goods? *Goods people use up in the production of other goods and services*
    H. Give an example from the brownie recipe of an intermediate good. *Answers will vary and include flour, sugar, butter, vanilla, cocoa, baking power and salt.*
    I. If a recipe calls for one-half cup of sugar and we want to double the recipe, or make twice as much, how many cups of sugar will we need? *One cup*

ASSESSMENT

Distribute a copy of Activity 10.3 to each student. Review the instructions. Allow time for the students to work in class or assign the activity as homework. Go over the answers with the students.

1. List two capital goods Jack and Jill will use to make the play dough. Explain why these are capital goods. ***Answers will vary and include spoon, stove and saucepan. These are capital goods because people produced them and other people use them to produce other goods and services.***

2. Who are the human resources making the play dough? ***Jack and Jill***

3. List two intermediate goods Jack and Jill will use. ***Answers include flour, salt, vegetable oil, cream of tarter and food coloring.***

VISUAL 10.1
BETTY'S BETTER BROWNIE RECIPE

½ cup of melted butter
1 cup of sugar
1 tablespoon of vanilla
2 eggs
½ cup of flour
⅓ cup of cocoa
¼ teaspoon of baking powder
¼ teaspoon of salt

Preheat oven to 350°F.
Mix butter, sugar, vanilla and eggs.
Add flour, cocoa, baking powder and salt.
Put in a greased 9-inch pan.
Bake for 20 to 25 minutes.
Serves 12.

VISUAL 10.2
BROWNIE RESOURCES

Items Used to Produce Brownies			
Natural Resources	**Human Resources**	**Capital Goods**	**Intermediate Goods**

ACTIVITY 10.1
MEASURING UP

Directions: Use the measuring cups you received and the dry ingredient to answer the following questions. Please explain your answers.

A. How many one-fourth-cup measures do you need for one full cup? How did you prove this?

B. How many one-third-cup measures do you need to fill a two-thirds-cup measure? How did you prove this?

C. How many one-eighth-cup measures must you use to make one-quarter cup? One-half cup? How did you prove this?

D. Which is larger: one-eighth of a cup or one-fourth of a cup? How did you decide this?

E. Write two sentences about fractions of a cup. Here's an example: *If I put a one-fourth-cup measure of dry ingredient in the bowl and a second one-fourth-cup measure of dry ingredient in the bowl, there will be two-fourths of a cup of dry ingredient in the bowl. This is the same as one-half cup.*

ACTIVITY 10.2
BROWNIE RESOURCES

Directions: Below is a list of items a local bakery uses when it makes brownies. Decide whether each item is an intermediate good or a natural resource, a human resource or a capital good. Write each item in the correct column of the table.

- baker
- chocolate powder
- eggs
- knife
- mixer
- oven
- pan

- salt
- spoon
- sugar
- timer
- vanilla
- vegetable oil
- water

Items Used to Produce Brownies			
Natural Resources	**Human Resources**	**Capital Goods**	**Intermediate Goods**

ACTIVITY 10.3
ASSESSMENT: JACK AND JILL'S GOOD DEED

Directions: Jack and Jill are making play dough for the children in their pre-school class. Read the recipe and answer the questions.

3   cups of flour
1½ cups of salt
3   cups of water
2   tablespoons of vegetable oil
1   tablespoon of cream of tartar
    Several drops of food coloring

Mix all ingredients in a large saucepan. Cook over medium-low heat while stirring with a spoon until the dough comes away from the edges of the pan or it becomes difficult to stir the dough. Remove from heat. Cool until you can handle the dough. Place the dough on the counter. Knead three to four times. Store in an airtight container.

1. List two capital goods Jack and Jill will use to make the play dough. Explain why these are capital goods.

2. Who are the human resources making the play dough?

3. List two intermediate goods Jack and Jill will use.

Lesson 11 - Plenty of Pennies

OVERVIEW

This lesson focuses on interest (economics) and percents (mathematics). The students use pennies to help them compute percents. They convert percent to decimals and figure interest amounts on savings or borrowed money. They role-play to understand that interest is payment for the use of money, and they discover that all financial choices have a cost.

CONCEPTS

Economics
Interest
Interest rate
Opportunity cost
Saving

Mathematics
Decimal
Percent
Problem solving
Using a formula

CONTENT STANDARDS

Economics
Standard 10
- **Benchmark 1 for 4th grade:** Banks are institutions where people save money and earn interest, and where other people borrow money and pay interest.
- **Benchmark 2 for 4th grade:** Saving is the part of income not spent on taxes or consumption.

Mathematics
Number and Operations
- Recognize and generate equivalent forms of commonly used fractions, decimals and percents.

Problem Solving
- Build new mathematical knowledge through problem solving.
- Solve problems that arise in mathematics and in other contexts.

Connections
- Recognize and apply mathematics in contexts outside of mathematics.

OBJECTIVES

The students will:
1. Explain that percent means part of a hundred.

2. Convert percent to decimals.

3. Use a formula to figure the interest a financial institution would pay on the principle amount in a savings account.

4. Define saving as giving up the purchase of goods and services today for purchases in the future.

TIME REQUIRED

120 minutes

MATERIALS

PART 1

1. Advertisements or advertising fliers from a magazine or local newspaper with promotions for a percent off the original price of a product

2. One hundred pennies in a plastic zipper bag for each student in half the class (The students will work in pairs. They should be at tables so that they can spread out their pennies.)

PART 2

3. One copy of Activity 11.1 for each student

PART 3

4. Visual 11.1

5. Enough copies of Activity 11.2 on blue paper so you have one Banker Card for each student in half the class

6. Enough copies of Activity 11.3 on white paper so you have one Depositor Card for each student in half the class

7. One copy of Activity 11.4 for each student

8. Ads or advertising fliers showing interest rates on loans (mortgage and car-dealer ads are good examples) and ads showing interest rates on savings accounts and certificates of deposit

ADDITIONAL RESOURCES

For additional curriculum connections, Web links, technology applications and suggested children's literature that will help you teach this lesson, go to
http://mathandecon.ncee.net/35/lesson11

PROCEDURE

PART 1

1. Show the students a newspaper or magazine advertisement for a good or service with a percent off the original price.

Discuss with the students what the percent off means in the ad. (Most students will know that it means the item is on sale, and you can buy it for less than the original price.)

2. Write 50% and 40% on the board. Explain to the class that if the ad says 50% off, buyers pay only half of the original price: They would save 50% and pay 50%. Ask the following questions:
    A. If you add 50% and 50%, what is your answer? *100%*
    B. If the ad says 40% off, how much of the original price do you pay? *60%*
    C. What percent would you save off the original price? *40%*
    D. If you add the 40% you saved and the 60% of the original price you paid, what is your answer? *100%*
    E. Point to the "%" and explain this means "per hundred." So if you say 1%, you mean one out of 100. If you say 50%, it means 50 out of 100. What does it mean to say 40%? *It means 40 out of 100.*

3. Divide the students into pairs. Tell them to look at the label in the neck of their partner's shirt to find the fiber content of the shirt. This is usually expressed as a percent. Tell the students to write on a piece of paper the numbers and words representing the fiber content. Allow time for the students to read and review the garment labels and write down their answers. *Answers will vary and include 100% cotton, 65% cotton and 35% polyester, and other combinations.*
(**Note:** Most children's shirts have a tag showing fiber content that ranges from 100% cotton to a combination of cotton and a manufactured fiber such as polyester to 100% polyester. Some shirts may have more than two fibers, but the total should always be 100%. You could bring a shirt with a label to use as an example.)

4. Select one or two pairs of students to come to the board and write the fiber content for both shirts.

5. Discuss the labels with the students. If a label says 100% cotton, the only fiber in the shirt is cotton. If it says 65% cotton and 35% polyester, then the fabric is made with 65% cotton and 35% polyester. Remind the students that the total is 100%. Allow the students who have different answers from those on the board to share their results.

6. Distribute 100 pennies to each student pair. If possible, have the students work at tables so they have enough room to spread out the pennies. Ask the students how many pennies they have. Allow time for them to count. Remind the students that 100 pennies equals $1.

7. Tell the students to put the pennies into groups of 10. Ask the following questions:
   A. How many groups of 10 were you able to make? *10 groups*
   B. What percent of 100 does each group represent? *10% of 100*

8. Tell the students to put the pennies in groups of 25. Ask the following questions:
   A. How many groups of 25 pennies were you able to form? *Four groups*
   B. What percent of 100 does each group represent? *25%*
   C. If 10 pennies represent 10% of 100 and 10 pennies equal one dime, then what percent of $1 is one dime? *10%*
   D. Twenty-five pennies equal a quarter, so what percent of $1 is a quarter? *25%*

9. Tell the students to divide their pennies into two equal groups. Ask the following questions:
   A. How many pennies are in each group? *50*
   B. What percent of 100 does each group represent? *50%*

10. Tell the students to put the pennies back in the plastic bag and close it. Collect the pennies.

PART 2

11. Review the Part 1 activities with pennies and percents. Tell the students to find a new partner, and give each pair a bag of pennies. If they are not already sitting at tables, they should go with their partner to the tables now.

12. Tell the students to group the pennies according to the years on the coins. These dates are the years when the pennies were minted, or manufactured from metal. Tell them to put all the pennies that were minted in the 1960s in a row; all the pennies minted in the 1970s in a row and all the pennies minted in the 1980s, 1990s and 2000s in individual rows. Ask the following questions:
   A. Do you have any pennies that are not in a row? *If some students have a few older pennies in their assortment, tell them to make another row for these pennies above the row for the pennies from the 1960s.*
   B. Ask one pair of students how many pennies they have in the 1970s row. *Answers will vary.* Ask the same pair to tell you what percent of their pennies are in the 1970s row. *The answer should be the same with the word "percent" added.* Write the answer on the board using the percent sign. Remind the class that percent means "part of a hundred" and the number you just wrote on the board is the part of 100 pennies that are in this pair's 1970s row. Ask the pair what percent of their pennies weren't minted in the 1970s. *The answer will depend on the first answer. Remind the students that the two percents total 100%.*

13. Give each student a copy of Activity 11.1 and go over the directions:
   Write the date of each penny in one of the squares on the grid. Make sure the dates are in chronological order, starting with the year of the oldest penny in the upper left corner. Write the year for each penny on a square, even if you

have more than one penny that was minted in the same year. Use the information in the completed grid to answer the questions. Show your work.

Allow time for the activity. Ask some students to share their answers.

14. Ask the pairs of students to combine their pennies with those of another pair to create sets of 200 pennies. Have them organize the pennies into 10 rows of 20 pennies, ignoring the dates this time. Ask the following questions:

   A. How many pennies now represent 100%? *200*

   B. How many pennies would represent 50%? *100*

   C. How many pennies would represent 25%? *50*

   D. How many pennies would represent 10%? *20*

   E. How many pennies would represent 1%? *Two*

15. Tell the students to put the pennies back in the plastic bag and close it. Collect the pennies.

Optional: For homework, assign the students to create a bar, circle or line graph representing their penny collection on the back of their activity sheet or on graph paper.

PART 3

16. Review Part I and II with the students using the following questions:

   A. What does percent mean? *Part of a hundred*

   B. If you have two dimes, what percent of $1 do you have? *20% because you have 20 cents out of 100*

   C. Ask a student to come to the board and write 10%. Remind the students that the percent sign means they should say "percent" after the number.

17. Tell the students that a percentage is based on 100, and it can also be written as a **decimal**. Write 0.01 on the board. Read

the decimal out loud and remind the students of the tenths and hundredths decimal places. Ask the following questions:

   A. Look at the decimal. How many pennies does it represent? *One penny*

   B. Would a volunteer please read out loud the number written on the board? *One-hundredth*

   C. What percent of 100 pennies does one penny represent? *1%*

   D. Would a volunteer go to the board and write 1% beside the decimal I wrote on the board?

   E. Do these two numbers express the same amount? *Yes, they both represent one out of 100.*

18. Write 25% on the board. Ask a student to read what you wrote. *25%* Write 0.25 on the board. Ask a student to read this. *Twenty-five hundredths* Ask the students whether these numbers represent the same part of 100. *Yes*

19. Ask the students to give examples of situations when they will use percent in the "real world." *Answers will vary but should include figuring how much the sale price lowers a regular price, how much they owe on a purchase with sales tax included and the share of votes a candidate receives in an election.* If no one says anything about figuring interest, tell them they will also want to know how to calculate **interest** they pay on a car loan or interest they receive on a **savings account**.

20. Ask the students if they know what the term **interest** means. If no one knows, say that interest is payment for the use of money. When people borrow money to buy a car or furniture, the lender will want some payment for allowing them to use the borrowed money temporarily. Display the loan advertisements and tell the students the payment for borrowed money is expressed as a percent called the **interest rate**. Have them note the interest rates for the loans in the ads.

21. Tell the students another type of interest rate is the interest per dollar a bank pays customers who have **savings** in a savings account or certificate of deposit. Savings is money people have not spent for goods and services or used to pay taxes today. It is money they are saving for future goods and services. The bank pays these customers, or savers, interest because the savers are allowing the bank to use their money. Display the advertisements for interest on savings accounts and CDs, and have the students note the interest rates.

22. Ask the students to pretend they have $100 in a savings account and are saving for a new computer. If the interest rate is 5% per year and they leave the money in the bank for one year, how much will they have in their savings account at the end of the year? Write the following formula on the board:

    Amount of Interest at the End of the Year = Interest Rate Per Year x Principal Amount Saved

    Help the students figure out the answer. The first step is to convert the 5% interest rate to a decimal.

    A. Ask a student to come to the board and write 5% as a decimal under the words "interest rate" in the formula. *0.05* The interest rate per year is five hundredths.

    B. Tell the students that **principal** is another word for the amount they started with, which, in this case, is the $100 deposited in the savings account.

    C. Ask the student at the board what amount should be written under the word "principal" and why. *$100, because this was the amount they started with in the savings account*

    D. Ask another student to come to the board and compute the interest. *I = 0.05 x $100, so amount of interest = $5*

    E. Ask if this is the total amount in their savings account after one year. *No, this is the amount of interest; they need another step to get the total.*

    F. Ask what they must do to determine the total amount in their savings account after one year. *Add the interest to the principal.*

    G. Ask the student at the board to find the total. Remind the student to use the formula you wrote on the board. *$100 + $5 = $105*

23. Ask the following questions:

    A. Why do people decide to save their money? *Answers will vary but should include they want to buy a good or a service and don't have enough money, so they decide to save until they have enough money for their purchase.*

    B. What is a benefit of depositing savings in the bank rather than keeping it hidden at home? *Answers will vary but should include money deposited in the bank will receive interest, and money hidden at home will not; savers will be able to satisfy their want more quickly because the interest will increase their total savings; money in a bank is safer than money kept at home.*

    C. What do savers give up when they decide to save? *They give up buying goods and services now so they can have future goods and services.*

24. Tell the students that the goods and services savers give up now for future goods and services are the savers' **opportunity cost**. Opportunity cost is the next best thing savers give up when they decided to save their money, so their opportunity cost would be the goods and services they could have bought today with their money.

25. Explain to the students that they are going to be doing some role-playing. Divide the students into pairs. Give one student in each pair a Banker Card from Activity 11.2. Give the other student in each pair a Depositor Card from Activity 11.3. Tell the students with the blue cards that they will be bankers and the students with the white cards that they will be customers who want to deposit some money in a savings account. Have the students

write their names on the first blank of their cards and then demonstrate their roles by talking through the steps in the following example using Visual 11.1:

• Assume that the student who is a banker gets a Banker Card that says "My bank is paying 6% interest on all savings deposits for one year."

• Assume that the student who is a depositor gets a Depositor Card that says "I want to deposit $125 in a savings account for one year."

• The depositor says to the banker "How much interest are you paying?"

• The banker says "6% interest. How much do you want to deposit?"

• The depositor says "$125."

• The banker figures the interest on the deposit — in this example, $125 x 0.06 or $7.50. The banker tells the depositor "You will earn $7.50 interest on your savings deposit for one year" and records $7.50 in the second blank on the Banker Card.

• The depositor records this interest amount — $7.50 — on the second blank of the Depositor Card and then figures the amount of total savings for the year — in this example, $7.50 in interest + $125 principal = $132.50 — and records the amount on the Depositor Card.

26. Tell the students to play their roles, use the formulas for finding interest, complete the math and fill in the blanks on their cards. When they have finished, go over their answers to make sure they did the math correctly. Collect the cards.

CLOSURE

27. After collecting the cards, ask the students the following review questions:

A. What does the word percent mean? *Part of 100*

B. How are percent and hundredths alike? *They are both parts of 100.*

C. If I have 100 books and give away 45, what percent of my books did I keep? *55%*

D. How would you express 33% as a decimal? *33 hundredths or 0.33*

E. If you borrow money to buy something, what do you pay the lender who lets you use the borrowed money temporarily? *Interest*

F. Who receives interest? *People who deposit money in savings accounts and people who lend other people money*

G. What is savings? *Income people have not spent for goods and services or used to pay taxes today*

H. If you put $200 in a savings account and leave it for one year and the interest rate is 6%, how much interest would you receive at the end of the year? *$12*

I. What would be the total in your savings account at the end of the year? *$212*

J. What is your opportunity cost when you save money? *The goods and services I could buy today*

ASSESSMENT

Distribute a copy of Activity 11.4 to each student. Tell the students to read and follow all directions. Allow time for the students to complete the questions. Go over the answers with the students.

1. Look at the table below, which shows the records of several savings accounts. Predict which depositor's account will have the most money at the end of one year, and circle the letter of this depositor. ***Depositor B***

2. Use the following formulas to complete the table:
   • Amount of interest at the end of a year = interest rate per year x principal amount
   • Total in account = principal amount + interest earned

3. The next best alternative savers give up to save their money is called their ***opportunity cost.***

4. What does the word percent mean? ***Part of a hundred***

5. If you borrow money from a bank to buy a car, what do you pay the bank for the use of its money? ***Interest***

6. What is 25% of 200? ***50***

7. 0.37 equals ***37%***

8. 47% equals ***0.47 or 47*** hundredths

Depositor	Interest Rate	Principal Amount	Interest Earned	Total in Account (at the end of one year)
A	6%	$79.00	$4.74	*$83.74*
B	8%	$86.00	*$6.88*	*$92.88*
C	11%	$48.00	*$5.28*	$53.28
D	15%	$65.00	$9.75	*$74.75*
E	23%	$53.00	*$12.19*	*$65.19*

VISUAL 11.1
ROLE-PLAY

BANKER CARD

I am Banker ___________________.
My bank is paying **6%** interest
on all savings deposits for one year.

You will earn ______________ interest
on your savings deposit for one year.

DEPOSITOR CARD

I am Depositor ___________________.
I want to deposit **$125** in a savings account
for one year. How much interest will I earn?

If you pay me ________ interest for using my
money for one year, at the end of the year the
total in my savings account will be ___________.

ACTIVITY 11.1
PENNY COLLECTION

Directions: Write the date of each penny in one of the squares on the grid on the next page. Make sure the dates are in chronological order, starting with the year of the oldest penny in the upper left corner. Write the year for each penny on a square, even if you have more than one penny that was minted in the same year. Use the information in the completed grid to answer the following questions. Show your work.

A. What percent of your pennies were minted in the 1970s?

B. What percent of your pennies were minted in the 1980s?

C. What percent of your pennies were minted in the 1990s and 2000s?

ACTIVITY 11.1 (continued)
PENNY COLLECTION

ACTIVITY 11.2
BANKER CARDS

<table>
<tr>
<td>

BANKER CARD

I am Banker _________________.
  My bank is paying **3%** interest
on all savings deposits for one year.

You will earn _____________ interest
on your savings deposit for one year.

</td>
<td>

BANKER CARD

I am Banker _________________.
  My bank is paying **4%** interest
on all savings deposits for one year.

You will earn _____________ interest
on your savings deposit for one year.

</td>
</tr>
<tr>
<td>

BANKER CARD

I am Banker _________________.
  My bank is paying **5%** interest
on all savings deposits for one year.

You will earn _____________ interest
on your savings deposit for one year.

</td>
<td>

BANKER CARD

I am Banker _________________.
  My bank is paying **6%** interest
on all savings deposits for one year.

You will earn _____________ interest
on your savings deposit for one year.

</td>
</tr>
<tr>
<td>

BANKER CARD

I am Banker _________________.
  My bank is paying **7%** interest
on all savings deposits for one year.

You will earn _____________ interest
on your savings deposit for one year.

</td>
<td>

BANKER CARD

I am Banker _________________.
  My bank is paying **8%** interest
on all savings deposits for one year.

You will earn _____________ interest
on your savings deposit for one year.

</td>
</tr>
<tr>
<td>

BANKER CARD

I am Banker _________________.
  My bank is paying **9%** interest
on all savings deposits for one year.

You will earn _____________ interest
on your savings deposit for one year.

</td>
<td>

BANKER CARD

I am Banker _________________.
  My bank is paying **10%** interest
on all savings deposits for one year.

You will earn _____________ interest
on your savings deposit for one year.

</td>
</tr>
</table>

ACTIVITY 11.3
DEPOSITOR CARDS

<table>
<tr><td>

DEPOSITOR CARD

I am Depositor _________________.
I want to deposit **$150** in a savings account for one year. How much interest will I earn?

If you pay me _________ interest for using my money for one year, at the end of the year the total in my savings account will be ___________.

</td><td>

DEPOSITOR CARD

I am Depositor _________________.
I want to deposit **$175** in a savings account for one year. How much interest will I earn?

If you pay me _________ interest for using my money for one year, at the end of the year the total in my savings account will be ___________.

</td></tr>
<tr><td>

DEPOSITOR CARD

I am Depositor _________________.
I want to deposit **$200** in a savings account for one year. How much interest will I earn?

If you pay me _________ interest for using my money for one year, at the end of the year the total in my savings account will be ___________.

</td><td>

DEPOSITOR CARD

I am Depositor _________________.
I want to deposit **$225** in a savings account for one year. How much interest will I earn?

If you pay me _________ interest for using my money for one year, at the end of the year the total in my savings account will be ___________.

</td></tr>
<tr><td>

DEPOSITOR CARD

I am Depositor _________________.
I want to deposit **$250** in a savings account for one year. How much interest will I earn?

If you pay me _________ interest for using my money for one year, at the end of the year the total in my savings account will be ___________.

</td><td>

DEPOSITOR CARD

I am Depositor _________________.
I want to deposit **$275** in a savings account for one year. How much interest will I earn?

If you pay me _________ interest for using my money for one year, at the end of the year the total in my savings account will be ___________.

</td></tr>
<tr><td>

DEPOSITOR CARD

I am Depositor _________________.
I want to deposit **$300** in a savings account for one year. How much interest will I earn?

If you pay me _________ interest for using my money for one year, at the end of the year the total in my savings account will be ___________.

</td><td>

DEPOSITOR CARD

I am Depositor _________________.
I want to deposit **$325** in a savings account for one year. How much interest will I earn?

If you pay me _________ interest for using my money for one year, at the end of the year the total in my savings account will be ___________.

</td></tr>
</table>

ACTIVITY 11.4
ASSESSMENT: PRACTICE WITH INTEREST

1. Look at the table below, which shows the records of several savings accounts. Predict which depositor's account will have the most money at the end of one year, and circle the letter of this depositor.

2. Use the following formulas to complete the table:
   - Amount of interest at the end of a year = interest rate per year x principal amount
   - Total in account = principal amount + interest earned

Depositor	Interest Rate	Principal Amount	Interest Earned	Total in Account (at the end of one year)
A	6%	$79.00	$4.74	
B	8%	$86.00		
C	11%	$48.00		$53.28
D	15%	$65.00	$9.75	
E	23%	$53.00		

3. The next best alternative savers give up to save their money is called their

____ .

4. What does the word **percent** mean?

5. If you borrow money from a bank to buy a car, what do you pay the bank for the use of its money?

6. What is 25% of 200?

7. 0.37 equals _________ %

8. 47% equals _________ hundredths

Lesson 12 - Birdly Exchange

OVERVIEW

This lesson focuses on barter, money and characteristics of money (economics) and fractions
and ratios (mathematics). The students will
role-play a bartering activity and participate
in trading simulations using feathers and
birdles (a form of paper money) as mediums
of exchange. They will compare their trading
experiences to decide why medium of exchange
is an important function of money. The students should have some grasp of fractions and
ratios, because the lesson introduces exchange
rate as a ratio and includes an activity in
which the students calculate the exchange rate
between U.S. dollars and birdles.

CONCEPTS

Economics
> Bartering
> Exchange rate
> Medium of exchange
> Money
> Trade

Mathematics
> Decimals
> Fractions
> Multiplication
> Problem solving
> Ratios

CONTENT STANDARDS

Economics
Standard 5
> • **Benchmark 1 for 4th grade:**
> Exchange is trading goods and services
> with people for other goods and services or
> for money.

Standard 11
> • **Benchmark 1 for 4th grade:** Money is
> anything widely accepted as final payment
> for goods and services.
> • **Benchmark 2 for 4th grade:** Money
> makes trading easier by replacing barter
> with transactions involving currency, coins
> or checks.
> • **Benchmark 5 for 4th grade:** Most
> countries create their own currency for use
> as money.

Mathematics
Number and Operations
> • Recognize and generate equivalent
> forms of commonly used fractions, deci-
> mals and percents.

Problem Solving
> • Solve problems that arise in mathemat-
> ics and in other contexts.

Connections
> • Recognize and apply mathematics in
> contexts outside of mathematics.

OBJECTIVES

The students will:
1. Give examples of the costs and benefits
   of bartering.

2. Explain the role of money as a medium
   of exchange and the usefulness of money
   in trade.

3. Compute exchange-rate problems using
   multiplication of decimals.

4. Explain why some mediums of exchange
   are easier to use than others.

TIME REQUIRED

120 minutes

MATERIALS

(**Note:** This activity requires advance preparation; you will prepare some of the activities and the students will prepare other activities. You will need to make and organize some materials ahead of time and be prepared to assist the students with their role-playing activities.)

1. Visuals 12.1 and 12.2

2. One copy of Activity 12.1, cut into cards

3. One copy of Activity 12.2 for each student in half the class

4. One copy of Activity 12.3 for each student in half the class

5. One copy of Activity 12.4, cut into cards and put into a small bag or basket

6. Twelve copies of Activity 12.5, cut apart

7. One copy of Activity 12.6 for each student in the class

8. One copy of Activity 12.7 for each student

9. Scissors

Optional: Calculator and feathers in appropriate colors for the feather-trading activity, badges or necklaces made of colored yarn to help the students identify themselves as natives or travelers.

ADDITIONAL RESOURCES

For additional curriculum connections, Web links, technology applications and suggested children's literature that will help you teach this lesson, go to http://mathandecon.ncee.net/35/lesson12

PROCEDURE

1. Ask the students if they have ever imagined traveling back in time to visit people and places of long ago. ***Answers will vary.*** Tell the students that they will be using a PTM (Pretend Time Machine) to travel back more than 300 years ago to an island far away to learn about the people of that time and place.

2. Ask the students to close their eyes and imagine time traveling as you read the following story:

    Some class members have an opportunity to travel on one of the first Pretend Time Machines. As they step out of the PTM, they arrive on the tropical island of Birdly. Beautiful trees, lush plants and colorful flowers surround them. They begin walking to explore the island and notice the amazing variety of birds overhead. There are tiny hummingbirds, golden finches, brightly colored parrots and macaws, big-beaked toucans and even a magnificent bird of paradise! No wonder this island is named Birdly. Suddenly, they come to a clearing in the road and notice the island natives are setting up for a market day. Each native family has a large blanket covered with goods, or objects that satisfy people's wants. The family members made or grew these goods. There are displays of ripe fruit, fresh vegetables and bread products. Some natives have live chickens and goats! Many families show their handmade jewelry and decorative cloth. As the student travelers tour the open market, they suddenly realize it is lunch time and they are starving! The ripe bananas, fresh pineapple and roasted corn look delicious. But the group has a major problem: Since they have gone back in time, the money in their pockets has no value on this island. How can they get lunch?

3. Tell the students to open their eyes. Ask them what the travelers could do to solve the lunch problem. ***Answers will vary. The students might suggest trading***

something the travelers have with them: a pencil, ring, toy or other good. (**Note:** If the students do not suggest trading, ask: Could we offer to trade something we have with us to get lunch? *Answers will vary. The students should say that this might work if everyone has items to trade.*)

4. Explain that these islanders trade for the goods they want at their market by **bartering**, which is the direct exchange of goods or services between people without the use of money. For the natives to barter successfully, each one has to want what the other has to trade. This idea is called double coincidence of wants. For example, if a native is bartering potatoes on market day, he may want to barter for something he cannot grow or make himself, such as cloth. His best trading partner would have cloth to barter and want his potatoes. In this way, he is trading for what he wants and both traders will be better off because of their direct exchange.

5. Tell the students that eight volunteers will role-play a bartering activity. Four volunteers will play the roles of native islanders with goods to offer on market day, and four will be student travelers who offer goods they brought with them in the PTM. Choose the eight students and ask them to stand in front of the class. Give each of the four natives one Native Barter Card and each of the four travelers one Traveler Barter Card, using the cards made from Activity 12.1.

6. Give the volunteers the following directions: Your job is to find another volunteer who has a good you want and will barter for a good the volunteer wants. This will satisfy your double coincidence of wants and enable both of you to barter successfully. You may barter more than once and with anyone, native or traveler, who will barter with you. You should continue bartering until everyone has found a partner who has a good they want and agrees to

barter. After trading cards, the partners should stand together to indicate a completed trade. The natives should try to barter for school supplies or toys, because these goods are new and interesting to them. The travelers should try to barter for food, because they are very hungry.

7. Start the bartering and give the volunteers about two minutes to find a trading partner.
(**Note:** Some volunteers will likely have difficulty trading because no one else desires their good. This difficulty will help the students see that bartering is not an easy process: Double coincidence of wants keeps volunteers from trading for just any good and motivates them to continue looking for a good that satisfies them.)

8. When the bartering time is up, thank the volunteers, collect their cards and ask them to return to their seats. Then discuss the activity with the class, using the following questions:
   A. Did everyone find a trading partner? *Answers will vary. Some students will have found a partner because someone else desired the good they offered. Other students will not have found a partner because no one else wanted their good and there was no double coincidence of wants.*
   B. Was it hard to find a trading partner? *Answers will vary. Some students will have matched easily while others who were unsuccessful may have become frustrated in the process of trading.*
   C. Would you want to barter regularly to get the goods you want? *Answers will vary. The students may say that bartering for all necessary goods would be too hard and time-consuming.*

9. Tell the students they will now travel to Birdly again in the PTM. Ask them to close their eyes as you read Part 2 of the story:
   During the next 100 years, the natives become tired of bartering for goods on

market day. It is difficult for them to find a double coincidence of wants every time they trade. Sometimes they must trade several times to be successful at bartering for what they want the most. So the natives decide to use something of value on their island as a **medium of exchange**: a good everyone will use to exchange for other goods or services. The island has beautiful birds with colorful feathers, and the natives use these feathers in making decorative clothing, arrow shafts, jewelry and fans. Many islanders collect feathers to display on "feather sticks," or small tree branches with the colorful feathers attached. The natives decide that feathers will be a great medium of exchange because feathers are easy to divide and carry, widely accepted and very useful. The islanders begin collecting and keeping bird feathers to use as money. A new group of travelers arrives on the island and comes upon another market day. They would love to trade for food and souvenirs. How can they solve their trading problem?

10. Tell the students to open their eyes. Ask them the following questions:

    A. What could the travelers do to solve their trading problem this time? *Answers will vary, but some students should suggest that the travelers could find or collect bird feathers to use at the market.*

    B. Do you think all feathers will have the same value in trade? *Answers will vary. The students might say that more unusual or harder-to-find feathers may have a higher value or that extremely common feathers may not be worth anything in trade.*

11. Tell the students that they will use bird feathers for a trading activity to continue the Birdly story. Half the class will play the roles of native islanders with goods to offer, while the other half will be student travelers who will trade for goods with feathers.

12. Explain to the students that before they begin trading, the class must set a monetary number value, or value as a unit of money, for each type of bird feather. Display Visual 12.1 and read the types of bird feathers and their characteristics. Ask the students to assign a monetary number value from 1 to 6 for each feather, based on its color and any unique features. Six will represent the highest value and one, the lowest. Tell the students to give each feather a different number for its monetary value. Record the number value for each feather in the third column of Visual 12.1. After completing the table, discuss the following:

    A. Which feather has the highest monetary value? Why? *Answers will vary. The students should say that the value reflects the feather's unique features or the fact that it is rarely found on the island.*

    B. Which feather has the lowest monetary value? Why? *Answers will vary. The students should say that the feather is more commonly found or lacks unique features.*

13. To begin the feather-trading activity, divide the class into two even groups: natives and travelers. Give the students scissors and crayons or markers, and have them prepare their trading cards, using the following instructions:

    Travelers: Give each student traveler one copy of Activity 12.2 to cut into cards. (If real feathers in appropriate colors are available, this would make the simulation even more realistic.) Now have them write the number value of each feather on the corner of the card, using the values on Visual 12.1. Tell them they will trade their feather cards for goods; they may trade some or all of their feathers during the activity. Have the students total the value of all their feathers and remember or write the amount on a scratch paper. *The total will be 21: 1 + 2 + 3 + 4 + 5 + 6.*

    Natives: Give each student native one copy of Activity 12.3 to cut into cards.

Collect the completed goods cards and sort them so you have 15 piles: one for each good. Set aside the Round 2 cards. Assign each native **one** good, and give the natives **all** the cards for their good. Tell them they will trade their goods cards to the travelers for feathers. They should notice that each good has a number value written in the corner of the card. They should trade their good only for a feather or feathers equal to this value. Have them total the value of their good before trading and remember or write the amount on a scratch paper. ***The total value will depend on which good the native has.***

14. Give the following instructions:
    • Remind the travelers that they have come to Birdly in the PTM and want food and souvenirs from the natives.
    • The natives will stand in a line across the front of the room, facing the travelers.
    • The natives will hold up one of their goods cards and tell the travelers the good they are offering and number value of their good.
    • The travelers will have three minutes to trade with the natives by exchanging feather cards for goods cards.
    • Any native who runs out of goods cards before the three minutes are up should sit down.
    • Travelers should sit down when they have finished trading.

15. Begin the three-minute trading round. When the round is over, ask the students to return to their seats. Have them recall the value of their feathers or goods before they started trading. Tell them to sort their cards into piles of feathers and goods and calculate the amounts they now have of each.

16. Ask several travelers to share the value of the goods they received in trade and the value of the feathers they have left. Ask several natives to share the value of the feathers they received in trade and the value of the goods they have left. Discuss

the following questions:
    A. Were you able to trade for every good or feather you wanted? Why? ***Answers will vary. Some students may say they couldn't trade for everything they wanted because they didn't have enough goods/feathers, or the particular good/feather they wanted wasn't available or the exchange would have been uneven.***
    B. Was it easy or hard to trade using feathers as money? ***Answers will vary. Some students may say they had problems because they didn't have feathers with the same value as the goods they wanted. Other students may have run out of goods/feathers too soon.***
    C. What might happen to feather trading if many of the birds left the island? ***Answers will vary and include feathers of these birds would likely become rare and more valuable; the trading process would become too difficult if enough birds disappeared from the island.***

17. After the students report on their trades, collect the goods and feather cards, and ask the students to help resort the goods cards back into one pile of cards for each good. Add a pile for each of the Round 2 goods cards.

18. Tell the students to close their eyes again as you read Part 3 of the Birdly story:
    Once again, the travelers board the PTM to travel to Birdly. When they arrive, it is about 100 years after their last visit. They look around for changes that have occurred on the island in the past century. The first change they notice is fewer trees and birds but more houses. As they continue to explore, they come upon another market scene. They observe many natives coming and going from a wooden structure on the edge of the marketplace. They walk closer to investigate and see a sign on the entryway that says "Bank of Birdly." Could it be that Birdly now has paper money and a banking system? They

peek inside and see islanders counting "birdles," a paper currency like U.S. dollars. Some natives have smaller versions of birdles, called "half birdles" or "quarter birdles." Yes, it's true! The natives are using a new money system on their island. The travelers follow several islanders back to the marketplace and look at the goods for sale. Natives are offering many items their families sold 100 years ago, but there are additions: decorations for the home, modern tools, premade feather sticks and money holders for carrying birdles. Again the travelers would like to buy delicious food or interesting souvenirs but have only U. S. money. What could they do?

19. Tell the students to open their eyes. Ask them how the travelers might solve this money problem. *Answers will vary. The students may suggest asking natives if they will accept U.S. money in trade instead of birdles or if the natives will still accept feathers. Someone may suggest a money exchange: U.S. dollars for birdles.*
(**Note:** If no one offers the following idea, ask: Do you think the Bank of Birdly could exchange U.S. dollars for birdles? *Answers will vary. Some students may know that people can exchange money from other countries at a bank.*)

20. Tell the students that they are in luck: The Bank of Birdly does exchange dollars for birdles, because the island has recently begun trading with the U.S. for goods. Introduce the term **exchange rate** as the price of one country's currency in terms of another country's currency. Tell the students that they will exchange U.S. dollars for Birdly birdles using the bank's exchange rate to get the proper number of birdles for each dollar.

21. Tell the students that the exchange rate at the bank is 1 to 4, or 1 dollar = 4 birdles. Write this on the board, then explain that, in mathematics, an exchange rate is sometimes expressed as a **ratio**. So

the exchange rate of 1 dollar to 4 birdles might also be stated as 1 dollar : 4 birdles, or simply 1 : 4. Write these ratios on the board, and then ask the following questions to practice using ratios:
   A. What is the ratio of 2 dollars to birdles? How did you solve this problem? *2 dollars = 8 birdles, or 2 : 8. Multiply both numbers in the ratio by 2.*
   B. Can you think of other ratio problems? *Answers will vary.*
   C. What is the ratio of teachers to the students in this class? *Answers will vary, depending on the size of the class, but the number of teachers : the number of students.*
   D. What is the ratio of girls to boys in this class? *Answers will vary but the number of girls : the number of boys.*

22. Display Visual 12.2 and work through the examples and the exchange problems with the class.
   A. Amount = $1.50 (dollars)
   $1.50 x 4 = ß6.00 (birdles)
   B. Amount = $1.75 (dollars)
   $1.75 x 4 = ß7.00 (birdles)
   C. Amount = $2.25 (dollars)
   $2.25 x 4 = ß9.00 (birdles)
   D. Amount = $3.75 (dollars)
   $3.75 x 4 = ß15.00 (birdles)

23. Ask the travelers to draw a Money Card from the bag or basket into which you put the cards made from Activity 12.4. The card they draw will determine how many U.S. dollars they brought with them on their trip to Birdly. Then ask the travelers to figure out how many birdles they should receive at the bank, based on the exchange rate of 1 : 4, and write this number on their Money Card.
   $2.00 = ß8.00, $2.50 = ß10.00,
   $2.75 = ß11.00, $3.00 = ß12.00,
   $3.25 = ß13.00, $3.50 = ß14.00,
   $4.00 = ß16.00, $4.50 = ß18.00,
   $4.75 = ß19.00, $5.00 = ß20.00,
   $5.25 = ß21.00, $5.50 = ß22.00

24. Tell the travelers to "visit the bank" (you) to exchange their dollars for birdles. Check the travelers' calculations, make the exchanges and give them the currency made from Activity 12.5.

25. While making the exchanges, ask a helper to hand out the goods cards, including the cards for Round 2, to the natives. Each native should receive **all** the cards for **one** good. Tell the natives that the number value for their good is the starting price, in birdles, for the good.

26. Give each student a copy of Activity 12.6.
• Tell the travelers to write their name and the number of birdles they have on the activity. *This number will vary based on the card they drew, and they will have 0 goods.*
• Tell the natives to write their name on the activity. Then they should calculate the total value, in birdles, of the goods they have to sell and write the answer on the activity. *The total will depend on which goods the natives have, and they will have 0 birdles.*

27. Remind the travelers that they have come to Birdly in the PTM and want to buy delicious food and interesting souvenirs from the natives. Give them the following instructions:
• The natives will stand in a line across the front of the room facing the travelers.
• The natives will hold up one of their goods cards and tell the travelers the good they are selling and its cost in birdles.
• The travelers will have three minutes to buy from the natives. They may spend some or all of their birdles on goods.
• Any native who runs out of goods cards before the three minutes are up should sit down.
• Travelers should sit down when they have finished buying.

28. Begin the three-minute buying round. When the round is over, ask the students to return to their seats and com-plete Activity 12.6 by totaling the value of the birdles or goods they have left and answering Question 3. *Answers will vary depending on the cards, but each student's total value should be the same before and after buying.*

29. Ask the students to share their results — purchased goods and value in birdles of goods sold — with the students sitting around them. Discuss these questions:
A. Were you able to buy or sell every good you wanted? *Answers will vary. Some students may say certain items were sold out or were too high-priced.*
B. Which is easier to use as money: paper birdles or real feathers? *Answers will vary, but most students will probably say that birdles were easier to use because they were more readily accepted, easier to handle, lasted longer, wouldn't break easily and divided into parts — half birdles and quarter birdles — more easily than feathers.*
C. Considering the goods and birdles you have now, are you more satisfied or less satisfied than when the buying round began? *Travelers with goods should be more satisfied now because they have some of the items they want. Natives might say they are less satisfied, but point out to them that with their birdles they can now buy the goods they want from other natives.*

CLOSURE

30. Ask the students to look over their activities for the trading and buying rounds, and discuss the following questions:

A. Give examples of some of the goods traded on the island of Birdly. *Potatoes, bread, pineapples, bananas, corn, chicken, arrows, fans, goats, cloth, tools, jewelry, money holders, home decorations, feather sticks*

B. The natives used bartering as their first method of trade. What is bartering? *The direct exchange of goods or services between people without the use of money*

C. Why was bartering difficult? *It was sometimes hard to make a direct trade, because travelers and natives needed a double coincidence of wants: Both had to want what the other was offering. They often had to trade several times to be successful at bartering and getting what they wanted.*

D. What is a medium of exchange? *A good that is generally accepted in exchange for other goods and services*

E. What did the natives use as their first medium of exchange? *Bird feathers*

F. Why did different types of bird feathers have different monetary number values? *Answers will vary and include some feathers were more colorful, unique, or rare than others, which increased their value in trade.*

G. Why do you think the natives changed to birdles as a medium of exchange? *Answers will vary and include birdles were easier to carry, more easily divided and could be reused. Feathers were less durable, harder to collect and keep, and not as convenient.*

H. What is an exchange rate? *The price of one country's currency in terms of another country's currency*

ASSESSMENT

Give each student one copy of Activity 12.7. Tell the students to read and follow the directions as they work individually. Allow time for completion or assign as homework. Go over the answers with the students when they have finished the assessment.

1. Canada is the first country on their trip. Bria and her family decide to exchange 100 of their U.S. dollars for Canadian dollars so they can go shopping. How many Canadian dollars should they get for their shopping trip? *The exchange rate is 1 : 1.20, so they will get $100 x 1.20 Canadian dollars, or 120 Canadian dollars.*

2. The second country they visit is Great Britain (England). They trade 50 U.S. dollars for British pounds. Do they have enough money to go on a tour of a castle that costs 20 pounds for the entire family? *Yes, $50 multiplied by .52 (the exchange rate) gives them 26 British pounds, which is more than enough to go on the tour.*

3. Their third stop is Japan. Bria's parents give her 20 U.S. dollars to spend here. Does she have enough to buy a souvenir hat that costs 3,000 yen? How about a souvenir book that costs 1,000 yen? *Bria gets 2070 yen for her $20 (20 x 103.5). This isn't enough for the hat (at 3,000 yen), but she can get the book (at 1,000 yen).*

4. Mexico is the final country on the trip. Bria and her family decide to eat dinner at a local restaurant and pay in pesos. Bria's dinner costs 60 pesos, her brother Jalen's meal costs 65 pesos and her mom and dad's dinners each cost 75 pesos. How much was the meal in pesos? How much would the meal have cost in U.S. dollars? *The family's meal totaled 275 pesos (60 + 65 + 75 + 75). It would have cost $25 U.S. dollars (275 pesos divided by the exchange rate of 11 pesos per dollar).*

VISUAL 12.1
FEATHER CHARACTERISTICS AND VALUE

Bird Feather	Characteristics	Number Value
Finch	Yellow, white, black Common	
Harrier	Cream, brown, black Common	
Loon	Black with white spots Somewhat common	
Macaw	Red, yellow Rare	
Parrot	Green, blue, red Bright colors, shiny	
Peacock	Blue and green "eye" Somewhat rare	

VISUAL 12.2
EXCHANGE RATES

Exchange rate is the price of one country's currency in terms of another country's currency.

The exchange rate at the Bank of Birdly is 1 dollar to 4 birdles. To exchange dollars for birdles, multiply the number of dollars by four.

Amount = $1.00 (dollar)
       x   4

    ß4.00 (birdles)

Amount = $1.25 (dollars)
       x   4

    ß5.00 (birdles)

Solve these exchange problems:

    A. Amount = $1.50 (dollars)

    B. Amount = $1.75 (dollars)

    C. Amount = $2.25 (dollars)

    D. Amount = $3.75 (dollars)

ACTIVITY 12.1
BARTER CARDS

Pineapple
Native
Barter Card

Yo-Yo
Traveler
Barter Card

Corn
Native
Barter Card

Rubber Ball
Traveler
Barter Card

Cloth
Native
Barter Card

Pencil
Traveler
Barter Card

Jewelry
Native
Barter Card

Rock
Traveler
Barter Card

ACTIVITY 12.2
FEATHER CARDS FOR TRAVELERS

Directions: Cut along the solid lines to make six cards, one for each feather. Write the feather's number value on the card, using the number value information on Visual 12.1.

ACTIVITY 12.3
GOODS CARDS FOR NATIVES

Directions: Cut along the solid lines to make 15 cards, one for each good.

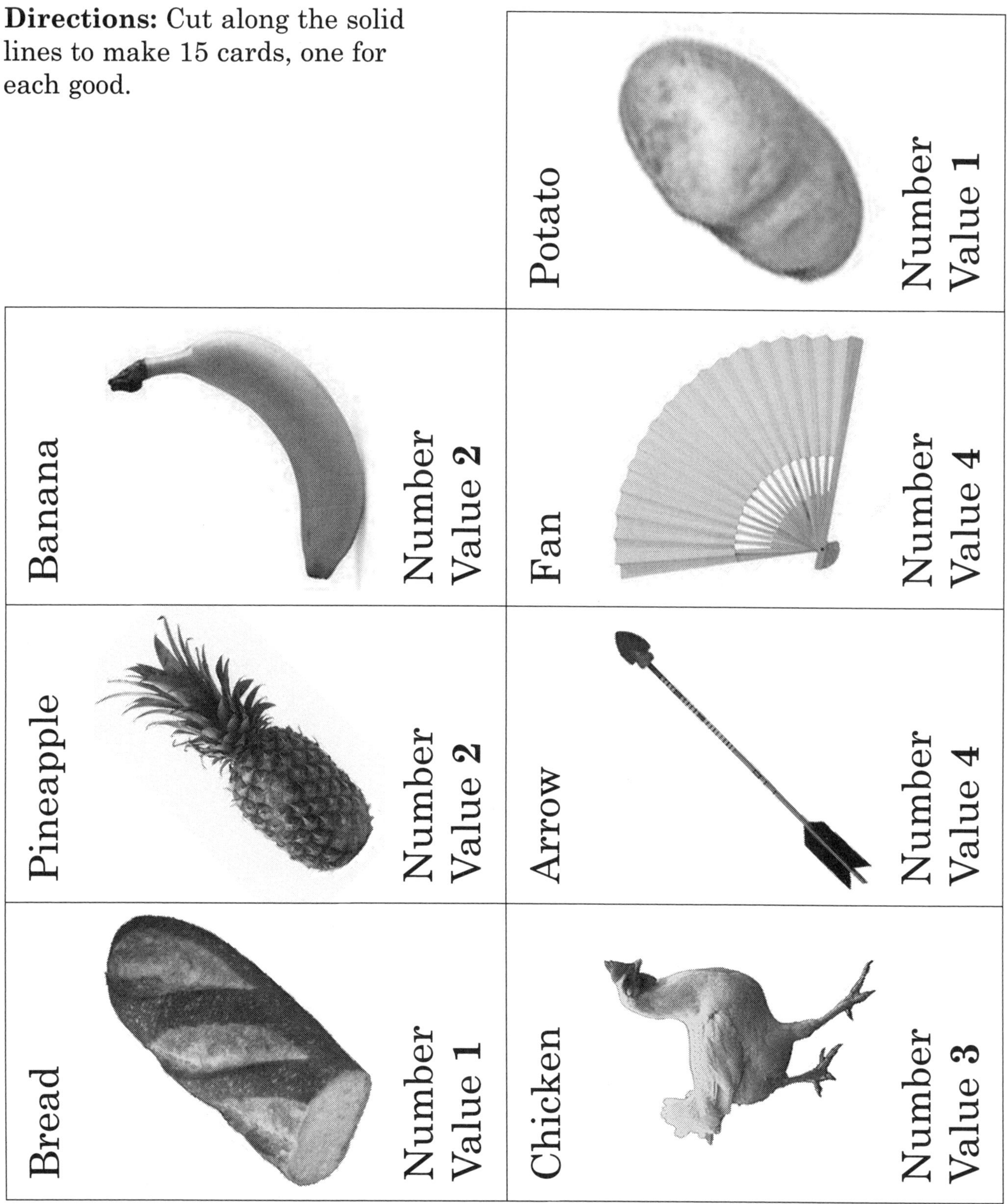

ACTIVITY 12.3 (continued)
GOODS CARDS FOR NATIVES

Jewelry — Number Value **5**	**Feather Stick (Round 2)** — Number Value **6**
Cloth — Number Value **5**	**Vase (Round 2)** — Number Value **6**
Goat — Number Value **4**	**Money Holder (Round 2)** — Number Value **6**
Corn — Number Value **3**	**Tool** — Number Value **5**

ACTIVITY 12.4
MONEY CARDS FOR TRAVELERS

$2.00 DOLLARS = ß_____ BIRDLES	**$2.50** DOLLARS = ß_____ BIRDLES
$3.00 DOLLARS = ß_____ BIRDLES	**$3.25** DOLLARS = ß_____ BIRDLES
$4.00 DOLLARS = ß_____ BIRDLES	**$4.50** DOLLARS = ß_____ BIRDLES
$5.00 DOLLARS = ß_____ BIRDLES	**$5.25** DOLLARS = ß_____ BIRDLES

ACTIVITY 12.4 (continued)
MONEY CARDS FOR TRAVELERS

$2.75 DOLLARS

=

ß_____ BIRDLES

$3.50 DOLLARS

=

ß_____ BIRDLES

$4.75 DOLLARS

=

ß_____ BIRDLES

$5.50 DOLLARS

=

ß_____ BIRDLES

ACTIVITY 12.5
BIRDLE CURRENCY

ß10   BANK OF BIRDLY   ß10   ß1/4   BANK OF BIRDLY   ONE-QUARTER BIRDLE

ß10   TEN BIRDLES   ß10   ß1/4

ß5   BANK OF BIRDLY   ß5   ß1/4   BANK OF BIRDLY   ONE-QUARTER BIRDLE

ß5   FIVE BIRDLES   ß5   ß1/4

ß1   BANK OF BIRDLY   ß1   ß1/4   BANK OF BIRDLY   ONE-QUARTER BIRDLE

ß1   ONE BIRDLE   ß1   ß1/4

ß1/2   BANK OF BIRDLY   ß1/2   ß1/2   BANK OF BIRDLY   ß1/2   ß1/4   BANK OF BIRDLY   ONE-QUARTER BIRDLE

ONE-HALF BIRDLE   ONE-HALF BIRDLE   ß1/4

ACTIVITY 12.6
BUYING GOODS WITH BIRDLES

Check one: _____ I am a traveler.   _____ I am a native.

1. At the beginning of this round, I have __________ birdles and

    __________ goods (valued in birdles), for a total value of __________ birdles.

2. At the end of this round, I have __________ birdles and

    __________ goods (valued in birdles), for a total value of __________ birdles.

3. Considering the goods and birdles you have now, are you more or less satisfied than before this round began? Why?

ACTIVITY 12.7
ASSESSMENT: HOW MUCH CAN YOU BUY?

Directions: Bria has won first place in an essay contest on economics. She and her family get a free trip to four countries and some spending money. Before they leave, Bria goes to the Internet and prints an exchange-rate table for the countries they are visiting. Can you help Bria and her family use the exchange-rate table?

Exchange Rate Table for U.S. Dollars		
Country	**Currency**	**For 1 U.S. dollar you get**
Canada	Canadian dollars	1.20 dollars
Great Britain	British pound	0.52 pounds
Japan	Japanese yen	103.5 yen
Mexico	Mexican pesos	11.0 pesos

1. Canada is the first country on their trip. Bria and her family decide to exchange 100 of their U.S. dollars for Canadian dollars so they can go shopping. How many Canadian dollars should they get for their shopping trip?

2. The second country they visit is Great Britain (England). They trade 50 U.S. dollars for British pounds. Do they have enough money to go on a tour of a castle that costs 20 pounds for the entire family?

3. Their third stop is Japan. Bria's parents give her 20 U.S. dollars to spend here. Does she have enough to buy a souvenir hat that costs 3,000 yen? How about a souvenir book that costs 1,000 yen?

4. Mexico is the final country on the trip. Bria and her family decide to eat dinner at a local restaurant and pay in pesos. Bria's dinner costs 60 pesos, her brother Jalen's meal costs 65 pesos and her mom and dad's dinners each cost 75 pesos. How much was the meal in pesos? How much would the meal have cost in U.S. dollars?

Glossary of Terms

Alternatives: options among which people can make a choice

Barter: direct exchange of goods or services among people without the use of money

Benefits of trade: increase in well-being after the voluntary exchange of goods and services

Budgeting: making a plan for managing income, spending and saving

Capital goods (resources): goods people produce and use to make other goods and services

Choice: a decision made among alternatives

Complementary goods and services: goods or services people typically consume together

Consumers: people whose wants are satisfied by using goods and services

Costs of production: the costs of all the resources a business uses in producing goods or services

Criteria: standards or measures of value that people use to evaluate something

Decision making: a process of choosing among alternatives

Demand: the schedule of the quantity of a good or service that people are willing and able to buy at different prices during a given time period, when income and prices of other items remain the same

Division of labor: jobs are divided among the workers so that each worker specializes in one part of the production process

Economic benefits: improvements in well-being associated with any economic action, good or service; for example, the increase in satisfaction from consuming something

Economic wants: desires that people can satisfy by consuming a good or service

Entrepreneurs: people who take risks to develop new products and services and start new businesses. Profit is income for entrepreneurs and is an incentive that encourages them to risk their money and resources.

Exchange rate: the price of one country's currency in terms of another country's currency

Goods: objects that can satisfy people's economic wants

Human capital: the skills, education and talent a person possesses

Human resources: the quantity and quality of human effort directed toward producing goods or services

Interest: the amount that a borrower of money must pay to the lender for the use of the lender's money

Interest rate: the percentage that a borrower must pay of the money loaned in return for the use of the money, usually expressed over a period of one year

Intermediate goods: materials that are used up in production and become part of the final good

Investment in capital: purchasing capital goods (equipment and buildings) that can assist people in producing goods and services

Law of demand: people are willing and able to buy a lower quantity of a good or service at a higher price and a higher quantity of a good or service at a lower price, when income and prices of other items remain the same.

Medium of exchange: a good that people generally accept in exchange for other goods or services

Money: anything widely accepted as final payment for goods and services (a medium of exchange)

Natural resources: "gifts of nature" that are present without human intervention

Opportunity cost: the next best alternative people give up when they make a decision

Productive resources: natural resources, human resources and capital goods available to make goods and services

Productivity: a measure of output compared to inputs during some time period

Profit and loss: difference between the total revenue a business receives and the total costs it pays for resources. If this number is positive, it is called profit; and if it is negative, it is called loss.

Revenue: total amount a business receives for selling a product or service

Savings: income people have not spent on consumption or taxes

Services: actions that can satisfy people's economic wants

Specialization: each worker focuses on one part of the production process

Trade/Exchange: voluntarily trading goods and services with people for other goods and services or for money

